Sandra Lieberman.

AN INTRODUCTION TO LLOYD'S MARKET PROCEDURES AND PRACTICES

TEXTBOOK FOR THE LLOYD'S INTRODUCTORY TEST

AN INTRODUCTION TO LLOYD'S MARKET PROCEDURES AND PRACTICES

TEXTBOOK FOR THE LLOYD'S INTRODUCTORY TEST

Edited by Lloyd's Training Centre

LONDON
WITHERBY & CO LTD
32–36 Aylesbury Street
London EC1R 0ET

Published 1986
1st Edition
2nd Edition 1987

MONUMENT
SERIES

ISBN 0 948691 22 0

Printed in Great Britain by
Witherby & Co Ltd
32–36 Aylesbury Street
London EC1R 0ET

Foreword to First Edition

The Introductory Test is a new departure for Lloyd's and one which I warmly support. I am, therefore, very pleased to contribute a foreword to this Text-book which can accompany the courses run in connection with that Test, and enable those who wish to do so to undertake some self-study.

I feel that the written word cannot replace, but only complement, the good tutor and I hope that as many individuals as possible will take advantage of oral tuition within their own firms or through Lloyd's Training Centre.

Peter Miller

Preface to First Edition

This book would not have been possible without the assistance given to the editors by individuals within the Lloyd's community and the tangible support from the Market Associations.

The Editors hope that this book will also be read by those seeking a knowledge of the business and practice of the Lloyd's Market. It cannot tell the full story since it relates only to the subjects of the syllabus but they hope it can take a valuable place amongst the other literature upon Lloyd's.

This book has been prepared for candidates for the Lloyd's Introductory Test, and as such provides a general description of the operations and procedures at Lloyd's covered by the areas of study listed in the syllabus. It is by no means exhaustive, and since it has been prepared by various individual contributors, it is not intended to be an authoritative statement.

Lloyd's Training Centre

London, December, 1985

Preface to Second Edition

The book has been extended and modified following publication of the first edition. Thanks are due to Market Association representatives for approving the text and to Corporation of Lloyd's staff for their assistance.

The section relating to the glossary has been extensively revised to provide clarification of the various terms defined. A number of sections have been amended and up-dated to reflect Lloyd's procedures and practices current at the time of publication of this second edition.

Lloyd's Training Centre

London, January, 1987

Lloyd's Introductory Test Syllabus

Purpose

To ensure that the new users of the Room have an understanding of the principles and practice of insurance particularly as it relates to the business of the Lloyd's Market, with particular reference to the roles of the Brokers and the Underwriters, and their respective responsibilities.

Candidates will be required to reach a satisfactory standard in a test which will seek to establish that the candidates have an adequate knowledge of the following topics:

A) *The basic purpose and nature of insurance and its value to the community.*

B) *Legal Principles Governing Insurance Transactions.*
   - i) utmost good faith and its significance in the relationship between Underwriters and Brokers.
   - ii) basic essential principles underlying every contract of insurance including the purpose and effect of warranties.
   - iii) the duties and responsibilities of a Broker and the simple basis of the law of agency.

C) *The Structure of the Lloyd's Market.*
   - i) the nature of Lloyd's, that is a society of individual Members operating in a market place and regulated by a Council.
   - ii) the Members of Lloyd's; their unlimited liability.
   - iii) the grouping of these Members in Syndicates and the basic role of Underwriting Agents.
   - iv) the position of Lloyd's Brokers in relation to the society.
   - v) the role and responsibility of an appointed Underwriter of a Syndicate.
   - vi) Market Associations.

D) *Lloyd's Market Practice.*
   - i) the method of conducting business in the Room including Brokers' and Syndicate numbers and pseudonyms.

ii) the way in which a policy is prepared and processed.

iii) the role and responsibility of Brokers in the handling of premiums.

iv) the role and responsibilities of Brokers in the settlement and payment of claims.

v) the role and responsibilities of Underwriting staff and the system of delegation and responsibilities within an Underwriting organisation.

vi) the nature and importance of Market Agreements.

vii) the particular responsibilities of Leading Underwriters within the Lloyd's system including the operation of Leading Underwriters Clauses.

viii) the importance of prompt and efficient transfer of premiums and payment of claims.

ix) the importance of prompt and efficient handling of claims.

All questions shall be based on English Law and Practice.

Candidates will not be required to have a knowledge of changes in legislation, including statutory instruments issued under existing Acts or insurance practice where changes occur less than two months prior to the test dates.

Contents

The way insurance operates—Insurable risks—Reinsurance—Review of main classes of business at Lloyd's. Main types of Reinsurance.

(i) Utmost good faith and its significance in the relationship between underwriters and brokers

(ii) Basic essential principles underlying every contract of insurance including the purpose and effect of warranties

Law of contract—Warranties—Insurable interest—Indemnity—Proximate cause—Subrogation—Contribution

(iii) The duties and responsibilities of a broker and the simple basis of the law of agency

Brokers—Outline of the law of agency—general principles—Broker's responsibilities to client—Broker's responsibilities to the Underwriter

(i) The nature of Lloyd's, that is a society of individual members operating in a market place and regulated by a Council

History of Lloyd's—The Lloyd's Market—Lloyd's Brokers—Members—Corporation of Lloyd's—Lloyd's Act 1982—Council of Lloyd's—Committee of Lloyd's—Self Regulation at Lloyd's–Corporation Departments

(ii) The members of Lloyd's; their unlimited liability

Security underlying policies at Lloyd's

(iii) The grouping of these members in syndicates and the basic role of underwriting agents

Grouping of members in syndicates—Duties and functions of underwriting agents—Members' agents—Managing agents

(iv) The position of Lloyd's brokers in relation to the Society requirements to be a 'Lloyd's Broking' firm—Lloyd's brokers

(v) The role and responsibility of an appointed underwriter of a syndicate

Abbreviations

A.O.A	Any one accident
A.O.O.	Any one occurrence
A.O.Occ	Any one occurrence
A.O.P.	Any one person or Any one Policy
A.O.V.	Any one vessel
A.P.	Additional premium
Appd	Approved
A.R.	All Risks
As orig.	As original or As original Conditions
B.D.I.	Both days inclusive
B.I.B.A	British Insurance Brokers' Association
Bord.	Bordereaux
C.C.	Civil commotions or Cancellation Clause
C/N	Cover Note or Credit Note
Coll Comm.	Collecting Commission
Comm.	Commission
Comp.	Comprehensive
Conds.	Conditions
C.P.A.	Claims payable abroad
D.O.C.	Driving other cars
Ded.	Deductible
e & e.a.	Each and every accident
e & e.c.	Each and every claim
e & e.l.	Each and every loss
e & e.o.	Each and every occurrence
Excl.	Excluding or Exclusion
Fac.	Facultative
Fac. Oblig.	Facultative Obligatory
F & A.P.	Fire and allied perils
f.c. & s	Free of capture and seizure
F.D.O.	For declaration purposes only
F.I.A.	Full Interest Admitted
F.P.A.	Free of Particular Average
F.S.R. & C.C.	Free of strikes, riots and civil commotions
G.A.	General Average
H.C.	Held Covered
H & M	Hull and machinery

I.B.A.	Insurance Broking Account
I.B.N.R.	Incurred but not reported
I.C.C.	Institute Cargo Clauses
L.A.C.C.	Lloyd's Aviation Claims Centre
L.C.T.F.	Lloyd's Canadian Trust Fund
LCTF	Lloyd's Canadian Trust Fund
L.A.U.A.	Lloyd's Aviation Underwriters' Association
L.I.B.C.	Lloyd's Insurance Brokers' Committee
L.A.U.A.	Lloyd's Aviation Underwriters' Association
Ll & Cos	Lloyd's and Companies
L.M.U.A.	Lloyd's Motor Underwriters' Association
L.P.O.	Lloyd's Policy Office
L.P.S.O.	Lloyd's Policy Signing Office
L/U	Leading Underwriter
L.U.A.	Lloyd's Underwriters' Association
L.U.A.A.	Lloyd's Underwriting Agents' Association
L.U.C.R.O.	Lloyd's Underwriters' Claims and Recoveries Office
L.U.N.C.O.	Lloyd's Underwriters' Non Marine Claims Office
n.a.	net absolutely or not applicable
N.C.A.D.	Notice of cancellation at anniversary date
N.M.A.	Lloyd's Underwriters' Non-Marine Association
N.R.B.	Net Retained Brokerage
Occ.	Occurrence
O.G.R.	Original Gross Rate
O.N.R.	Original net rate
P.A.	Personal Accident or Particular Average
P.A.N.	Premium advice note
P. & I.	Protection and Indemnity
P.P.I.	Policy Proof of Interest
Q.S.	Quota Share
R.C.C. & S.	Riots and civil commotions and strikes
Retn.	Retention
R/I	Reinsurance
R.P.	Return Premium, Return of Premium
S.A.N.R.	Subject to approval no risk, Subject acceptance no risk
T.B.A.	To be advised; To be agreed
T.L.O.	Total loss only
T.O.	To Oblige
T.O.C.	Terms of Credit

T.O.R.	Time on Risk
U.E.P.	Unearned Premium
U.N.L.	Ultimate net Loss
Unltd	Unlimited
W/d	Warranted
w.e.f.	With effect from
w.p.	without prejudice
Wtd	Warranted
W/W	Worldwide
Xs. Loss	Excess of Loss, Excess Loss

Glossary of Terms

(N.B. This glossary contains some terms which are additional to those referred to in the text.)

Accountant's report
An annual report submitted to the Council in accordance with the Lloyd's Brokers' Accounts and Solvency Regulations.

Active Underwriter
Means the person at the underwriting box, or deemed by the Committee to be at the underwriting box, with principal authority to accept risks on behalf of the members of a syndicate managed by a managing agent.

Additional deposit
Security/ies added to the Lloyd's deposit to meet Committee requirements.

Advice cards
Cards issued to Lloyd's underwriters by Lloyd's Policy Signing Office (LPSO) showing punched and printed information relating to the transaction being processed (eg original premium, claim, additional premium).

Annual Subscriber
An individual employed by a Lloyd's broker or Lloyd's underwriting agency who has been nominated and elected as an annual subscriber, and who is thus permitted to enter the Room to transact insurance business in the name of his/her employer.

Approved accountant(s)
All accountants' reports submitted to the Committee in respect of Lloyd's Brokers' Accounts and Solvency Regulations must only be given by an accountant or firm of accountants approved by the Council.

Assignment
The passing of beneficial rights from one party to another. A policy or certificate of insurance cannot be assigned after interest has

passed, unless an agreement to assign was made, or implied, prior to the passing of interest. An assignee acquires no greater rights than were held by the assignor, and a breach of good faith by the assignor is deemed to be a breach on the part of the assignee.

Associate
An individual not being a member of the Society who has been nominated and elected as an associate, and who is thus permitted to enter the Room to provide services for underwriters (ie accountants, loss adjusters, solicitors, etc).

Attachment date
The date the underwriters come on risk (Inception date).

Audit or Solvency Reserves
Non-marine practice, in the event of property underinsurance, a claim payment is scaled down in proportion to the degree of underinsurance. In marine insurance average means a partial loss, and the terms used are particular average and general average.

Average
Where, in the event of underinsurance, a claim payment is scaled down in proportion to the degree of underinsurance. Average in marine insurance means partial loss. Particular average and general average are forms of partial loss.

Binding authority
An agreement under which a "coverholder" (usually a firm of insurance brokers) is authorised in accordance with the terms and conditions laid down therein, both to accept risks on behalf of those underwriters at Lloyd's subscribing to the agreement and to issue documents evidencing cover which bind those underwriters without their prior approval. A "Limited Binding Authority" allows the coverholder to issue documents evidencing that risks have been accepted on behalf of underwriting members only after they have been accepted (and rated if appropriate) by the leading underwriter or as provided on the slip.

Brokerage
The commission received by a broker for placing insurance risks

on behalf of the insured. In practice it is paid to the broker, by the underwriter out of the gross premium. However, the expression also means the business of the broker.

Brokers' daily statement
A document produced for brokers giving a daily summary of monies due to or from underwriters as a result of transactions processed under Central Accounting.

Cedant
One who cedes a risk, to his reinsurers.

Cede
To transfer risk from a direct insurer to his reinsurer.

Central Accounting
The arrangements whereby the accounting and settlement of premiums and claims and associated items between Lloyd's brokers and Lloyd's underwriters is centralised (it does not apply to UK motor business).

Certificate of Insurance
Evidence, in the form of a certificate issued in the name of the insurer, that an insurance contract exists; for example, that there is a motor insurance in force which complies with the terms of the Road Traffic Acts.

Cession
The particulars of a risk being transferred by an insurer to another.

Claims Payable Abroad (CPA) and Settlement of Claims Abroad (SCA)
Lloyd's policies/certificates, mainly marine cargo, which provide for the adjustment of claims at destinations abroad are said to be CPA. When claims arise and are adjusted and settled by Lloyd's Agents they are handled through the SCA system controlled by the SCA Office of the Agency Dept.

Closed Year
A year of account to which no further adjustments are to be made and final accounts or profits statements can be prepared. This can be done only after providing for all outstanding claims by way of reinsurance to close. At Lloyd's the closed year is usually the third year of account.

Co-insurance
Where two or more insurers share a single risk. Each co-insurance is a separate contract with the insured. In the USA the word applies to non-marine average.

Common Law
The law which has been founded upon immemorial usage, established custom, and legal decisions, as distinct from Statute Law.

Condition
A part of a contract which must be complied with by one party or the other.

Connected or Associated Name
Connected or Associated Names are individuals who, whilst not strictly qualifying as Lloyd's Working Names, are employees or principals of Lloyd's underwriting agencies or Lloyd's brokers, holding or subsidiary companies of such agents or brokers, or other companies with the same group, or branch offices of such agents or brokers, where it can be proved that for five years immediately prior to election their personal employment has been, and is likely to continue to be, of benefit to the Lloyd's market.

Continuing means undertaking
An undertaking signed by a member agreeing to maintain wealth at a certain level.

Contract of Insurance
An agreement between an insurer and one or more parties, called the insured, whereby the insurer undertakes in return for the payment of a consideration, called the premium, to pay to the insured a sum of money or to grant certain compensation on the happening of a specified event.

Contribution
The division of a loss between insurers where two or more cover the same insured and the same risk so as to cause over-insurance by double insurance. Contribution arises from the principle of indemnity and ensures equitable distribution of losses between insurers.

Co-ordinating agent
One of a member's underwriting agents (where the Name under-writes through more than one member's agent) nominated by the member to co-ordinate certain of his underwriting affairs.

Coverholder
A broker (not necessarily a Lloyd's broker) or agent authorised by underwriters to bind business within agreed limits and conditions on underwriters' behalf and to issue insurance documentation.

Cover Note
A document issued as evidence that insurance has been granted pending the issue of the policy. (For motor insurance the cover note includes a certificate of insurance to comply with Road Traffic Act requirements and there is usually a time limit of 15 or 30 days).

Declaration
A statement signed by the proposer (insured) at the foot of a proposal form, certifying accuracy of the information given to the best of their knowledge and belief. It may also be a risk declared to underwriters as attaching to an open cover.

Declaration of default
Formal resolution by Committee of Lloyd's that a member has failed to meet his obligations as an underwriting member.

Declinature
Refusal of an insurer to accept or renew a proposal for insurance.

Deductible
An amount or percentage, specified in a policy, which is deducted from a claim. The English terminology is excess.

Deemed Attachment Date
The date entered on the broker's slip by the leading underwriter to provide a point from which the period allowed in the Terms of Credit Scheme will operate for marine and aviation risks.

Deposit trust deed
A legal document signed by the member appointing the Corporation of Lloyd's as trustee of the Lloyd's deposit held as security for his underwriting liabilities.

Direct assured business
Where the "insured" negotiates personally with the Lloyd's broker or motor business as defined below.

'Direct' dealing motor business
An arrangement whereby UK non-Lloyd's brokers deal direct with Lloyd's motor underwriters.

Disclosure
The duty of the insured and his broker to tell the underwriter every material fact before acceptance of the risk.

E & O E
Errors and omissions excepted, and is shown at bottom of brokers' credit, debit or covernotes.

Earned Premium
That portion of the insurance premium relating to the accounting period in question or premium to a particular date.

Endorsement
Any writing on or addition to a policy, an addition to the printed wording, which changes or varies terms of or parties to the contract.

Exception
A peril or contingency specifically excluded from the cover of the policy.

Excess
The first portion of a loss, being an agreed percentage or fixed sum, which the insured agrees to bear or a portion another insurer is bearing.

Excess of line reinsurance
A reinsurance to cover that part of the original underwriter's acceptance which is in excess of his retained line.

Excess of loss reinsurance
A reinsurance to cover that part of a loss paid by the reinsured which is in excess of an agreed amount and then pays up to the limit of the policy.

Experience
The past claims record of an insured or reinsured.

External member
A member of the Society who is not a working member of the Society.

Fac/oblig
Facultative/obligatory. A reinsurance term for a contract where the reinsured can select which risks he cedes to the reinsurer, but the reinsurer is obliged to accept all cessions made.

Facultative Reinsurance
An individual reinsurance negotiated and placed individually.

First Loss
The first part of an insured loss—often the deductible of an insurance or reinsurance.

Franchise
Where an insurance or reinsurance only covers losses exceeding a certain agreed amount or percentage, the full loss then being paid without deduction.

Gross Premium
The full amount of premium ignoring taxes or deductions.

Gross Premium Underwriting Limit
The maximum amount of business which a member may underwrite based on the levels of his means and deposits. The limit is allocated to syndicates in proportions agreed between the member and the members' agent.

Insurance Brokers (Registration) Act 1977
An Act providing for the registration of individual insurance brokers and the listing of bodies corporate, and for regulating their professional standards.

Insurance Brokers Registration Council
The regulatory body set up under the Insurance Brokers (Registration) Act, 1977.

Insurance Broking Account (IBA)
A bank account held by a broker which must be separately designated to receive monies arising from insurance transactions payable from or to clients or underwriters.

Incidental non-marine
Non-marine risks placed with incidental non-marine syndicates run by marine underwriters within the marine market.

Incidental Marine Business
Marine risks placed with non-marine syndicates, who use a specific audit code for identification purposes.

Indemnify
To make good a loss suffered by the insured.

Indemnity
Indemnity is the legal principle which ensures that a policyholder is restored to the same financial position after the loss as he was immediately prior the loss.

Insurable interest
The insured's financial interest in the subject matter of the insurance. A policy where the insured is without such interest is unenforceable (but see P.P.I. policies).

Leader
An underwriter whose judgement is so respected by other underwriters that they will follow his lead in accepting a risk. His syndicate will appear first on the slip.

Leading underwriter's agreement
An agreement which allows for certain changes in conditions to be agreed by the leader without the agreement of all subscribing underwriters.

Liability insurance
Insurance to cover the legal liability of the insured to the extent of such liability, but subject to any limitations expressed in the policy.

Line
The sum or percentage written on a broker's slip on behalf of the syndicate of names for whom he acts which establishes the proportion of the risk accepted by an Underwriter. The written line is the maximum the underwriter is prepared to accept and the signed line, the amount required to complete the order subject to the maximum of the written line.

Line Slip
A facility off which a broker may declare individual insurances subject to acceptance by leading underwriters on behalf of following underwriters.

Line stamp
A rubber stamp used by a Lloyd's underwriter. It incorporates the syndicate's pseudonym and number and is impressed on the broker's slip by the underwriter who inserts his line and reference and initial.

Lloyd's Annual Solvency Test
An Annual test to ensure sufficiency of assets to meet future underwriting liabilities.

Lloyd's broker
A partnership or body corporate permitted by the Council to broke insurance business at Lloyd's.

Lloyd's Central Fund
A fund established in 1926 to protect policyholders in case any member of Lloyd's fails to meet his underwriting liabilities.

Lloyd's Deposits
Investments, cash, bank or insurance company guarantee or Letter of Credit held in the sole name of the Corporation of Lloyd's as trustee for an individual underwriting member under a deposit trust deed executed by the member and on which the member or beneficial owner is entitled to receive any relevant dividends or interest.

Long tail
A term used to describe a risk that may have claims notified or settled long after the risk has expired. So that he can close the underwriting account for the year it is often necessary for an underwriter to arrange reinsurance protection to cover claims which may arise after the account has been closed. A term used to describe risk covered as those of liability rather than physical damage.

LPSO number and date
The number and date allocated to a transaction signed in LPSO. This is an LPSO reference which is unique to any one transaction.

Managing Agent
A managing agent is a person who is permitted by the Council in the conduct of his business as an underwriting agent to perform for an underwriting member one or more of the following functions
(i)   underwriting contracts of insurance at Lloyd's
(ii) reinsuring such contracts in whole or in part
(iii) paying claims on such contracts.

Market agreement
An agreement between and subscribed to by all underwriters in a certain section of the Lloyd's market.

Market associations
Associations representing respectively:–
Marine underwriters (Lloyd's Underwriters' Association)
Non-marine underwriters (Lloyd's Underwriters' Non-Marine Association)
Aviation underwriters (Lloyd's Aviation Underwriters' Association)
Motor underwriters (Lloyd's Motor Underwriters' Association)
Underwriting agents (Lloyd's Underwriting Agents' Association)
Lloyd's brokers (Lloyd's Insurance Brokers' Committee of BIBA)

Material fact
Any fact or circumstance which would affect the judgement of an underwriter in considering whether he would accept the risk or not and at which rate of premium.

Material representation
A statement made to the underwriter before acceptance of risk which is material to his decision in accepting and rating the risk.

Members' agent
An underwriting agent who acts in all respects for the Name except the managing of the syndicate.

Minimum margin of solvency
The minimum amount by which insurers' free assets must exceed their reserves for future liabilities.

Misrepresentation
A mis-statement of fact made by the insured or his broker to the underwriter, before acceptance of the risk, which misleads the underwriter in assessing the risk. If the representation is material and amounts to misrepresentation it is a breach of utmost good faith.

Moral Hazard
The risk arising from the character and management style of the insured or his employees.

Name
An underwriting member whose name appears on the list of those participating in any syndicate at Lloyd's.

Net absolute
Premium is payable net of all discount, tax, etc. including any over-rider applicable. Return premiums are usually paid on this basis.

Net line
The amount of the original line retained by the reinsured.

Net retained brokerage (NRB)
Brokerage retained by a broker after allowances to other parties have been deducted. However, for margin of solvency purposes, NRB includes all fees, income and charges receivable in respect of services rendered or expenditure incurred.

Non-disclosure
Failure by the insured or his broker to disclose a material fact or circumstance to the underwriter before acceptance of the risk.

Non-underwriting member
This category enables Council to retain jurisdiction over members until underwriting is wound up.

One outlet rule
A Lloyd's broker must be able to demonstrate, and be able to continue to demonstrate, that it can reasonably expect not to be unduly reliant in any one financial year upon any one body corporate carrying on insurance business or any one Lloyd's syndicate in the placing of its business.

One source rule
A Lloyd's broker must be able to demonstrate, and be able to continue to demonstrate, that it can reasonably expect to secure business from a broad spread of sources so that it is not unduly reliant in any one financial year upon one predominant source of business.

Outward Reinsurance
The reinsurances of Lloyd's syndicates.

Overplacing
Placing more than 100% of Lloyd's order.

Personal reserve
A fund retained by the underwriting agent on behalf of a member as security for his underwriting liabilities.

Physical Hazard
The risk associated with the subject matter of insurance.

Pool Schemes
Various arrangements for processing very small premium or claim entries which are pooled and shared amongst syndicates rather than being applied to the correct syndicates.

Portfolio transfer
A transfer of an agreed portfolio from a specified date whereby the reinsurer accepts a premium representing the unexpired portion of risks already ceded, and liability for outstanding losses not yet settled in order that the accounting function may be transferred to a current period.

P.P.I. Policies
In marine insurance it has become customary to issue policies
where there is no need to establish insurable interest, such policies
are termed P.P.I. (Policy Proof of Interest) policies.

Premium
The amount paid to an insurer or reinsurer in consideration of his
acceptance of risk.

Premium limit
The total amount of gross premium income (1988) which may be
underwritten by an individual Name or syndicate in any one
calendar year, this is monitored by syndicate, class and in total.

Premium limit excess
The amount by which a member's premium income exceeds the
agreed premium limit may require the provision of a temporary
deposit as additional security.

Premium limit undertaking
An undertaking signed by a member not to exceed his premium
limit.

Premium Trust Fund (PTF)
A trust fund required under the United Kingdom Insurance
Companies Acts, into which all premiums and other underwriting
monies must be paid.

Premium Reserve
A portion of premium, otherwise due to a reinsurer, retained by
the re-assured for a pre-determined period. This may be a
statutory requirement.

Premium transfer
Syndicate accounting is on an annual basis but some longterm
insurance contracts run for more than 12 months. Where the
premium paid in the first year relates in part to subsequent years a
transfer may be arranged at the end of the year to carry forward
the relevant premium to the subsequent underwriting year's
account. The operation becomes a book entry only.

Profit commission
A commission payable on the profit generated under an insurance or reinsurance contract as an encouragement to maintain the flow of profitable business. It is also a commission payable by a Name to the Member's agent and shared with the Managing agent. It is calculated on the balances available at 36 months on a syndicate by syndicate basis, the basis of calculation varies from syndicate to syndicate.

Proposal
An application by a proposer for insurance, on a printed form. The "proposer" becomes the insured when the application has been accepted and the contract brought into existence.

Prospectus
A form, which is often part of the proposal form, giving details of the cover available with particulars of extra benefits and rebates.

Quota share reinsurance
A reinsurance agreement whereby the reinsured cedes a pre-determined proportion of all business (or specified part thereof) to his reinsurers.

Reinsurance (R/I)
The reinsurance of an insured risk. The laying off of a risk by an insurer to protect his particular liability and maintain liquidity.

Reinsurance to close
A premium paid usually at the end of the third year of an account by the members of the syndicate to the members of a succeeding year who then assume the outstanding liabilities.

Related insurance broker
An insurance broker in the same group of companies as a Lloyd's broker.

Representation
A statement of fact made by the insured or his broker when negotiating an insurance with the underwriter.

Retention
The amount retained by a reinsured when effecting a reinsurance.

Retrocession
The laying off of liability accepted by way of reinsurance for the same reasons as reinsurance.

Risk
A fortuity, it does not embrace inevitable loss. The term is used to define causes of loss covered by a policy.

Rota Committee
A committee established to interview applicants for underwriting membership or for admission as a Lloyd's broker or underwriting agent.

Run-off
The continued operation of a portfolio once the decision to cease accepting new business or renewals takes place. It can relate both to a whole entity or a portfolio or individual insurances.

"Scratching"
Initialling an agreement.

Security
The underwriters or companies subscribing to a risk.

Separation
A procedure to separate the premium payment from the policy signing procedure. A slip can be signed to comply with the terms of credit requirements and the policy can be prepared and signed at a later date.

Short tail
A term used to describe a risk in respect of which all claims are likely to be advised and settled within the period of cover or shortly after the cover has expired normally confined to physical damage risks.

Signed line
The amount of an underwriter's line under the completed slip. This is shown in the policy in the Table of Definitive Numbers.

Signing and accounting (S & A)
A procedure at LPSO whereby accounting procedures are conducted concurrently with the policy signing procedure.

Signing slip
The broker's slip used for submitting details to LPSO for signing and accounting. This can be the original slip, certified photocopy of the original slip or an initialled copy of the original slip.

Slip policy
A slip policy is a broker's slip which is made into a policy by the attachment of a special form; the purpose being to provide for those cases where the insured or reinsured does not require a formal policy.

Special reserve fund
An arrangement under the Income Tax Acts whereby a proportion of underwriting profit and certain investment income can be placed to reserve with relief from or deferral of higher rate tax. The fund is available for relief for future losses only.

Special settlements
A scheme under the Cental Accounting arrangement where settlement takes place within 3 working days of entries being "taken down" at LPSO.

Stamp allocated capacity
The amount of premium income which a syndicate may underwrite representing the sum of the allocations of premium limits made by participating members to that syndicate.

Standard slip
The slip used in the Lloyd's market by brokers which has a standard format. Slips are pre-printed in the standard format, so that the positioning of the relevant information is constant.

Stop Loss reinsurance (Excess of Loss Ratio)
A form of protection which makes it possible to limit the loss ratio on a year of account to an agreed percentage of the original insured's premium income on business protected. Personal stop loss reinsurances are also used by individual members to obtain a measure of protection against an overall underwriting loss on any one year of account.

Subrogation
The right of the underwriter to take over the insured's rights following payment of a claim to recover the payment from a third party responsible for the loss. Limited to the amount paid on the policy.

Substitute
A person granted a ticket of admission to the Room in order to conduct the business of insurance on behalf of the member, annual subscriber or associate by whom he is employed.

Surplus line business
Business surplus to the capacity of the local licensed market, especially important in the U.S.A. or for which no filed regulatory rates exist.

Surplus line reinsurance
A reinsurance where the excess of the reinsured's retention is ceded. The reinsurers will normally base his participation on the retention of the ceding insurer but once accepted the reinsured and reinsurers pay their proportion of losses arising.

Syndicate constitution or Syndicate stamp
A document detailing the members, and their shares, who underwrite on a particular syndicate.

Syndicate Run-Off
The administration of a disbanded syndicate involving settlement of claims and eventual reinsurance when the outstanding claims can be accurately assessed to the satisfaction of another Lloyd's underwriter usually for a premium, to take over the remaining liabilities allowing the account to be "closed".

Syndicate reinsurance
Outgoing reinsurances placed on behalf of Lloyd's underwriters through Lloyd's brokers with other Lloyd's syndicates or insurance companies. LPSO processes reinsurance premiums and claims passing between the reinsured underwriter and his Lloyd's broker.

Syndicate stamp
See "Syndicate constitution".

Table of definitive numbers
The schedule of syndicate numbers showing those syndicates participation which is attached to a Lloyd's policy.

Technical reserves
Funds held by an insurer/reinsurer to pay for the liabilities of a portfolio of business, they will usually include an allowance for premium reserves and claim reserves plus I.B.N.R.

Third party liability
Liability incurred by the insured to another party under common or statute law.

Treaty
A reinsurance contract usually effected to cover the whole or a certain section of the reinsured's business.

Treaty scheme
A procedure used in LPSO to process transactions for some types of treaty reinsurance. These will usually be processed on a quarterly basis. Settlements of debits and credits will be made on a balance basis, although separate amounts for premiums and claims etc must be recorded.

"Twenty percent" rule
Shareholdings by both insurance interests and non-insurance interests in Lloyd's brokers are controlled. For shareholdings by insurance interests the general rule is that shareholdings in a Lloyd's broker by non-Lloyd's insurance interests (whether directly or through other companies or persons in the groups) be limited to 20% of the total share capital and in the case of unquoted companies such shareholding should be in non-voting shares. Any new holders of 20% or more of the total share capital (where specifically agreed) should give a Letter of Undertaking in the prescribed form regarding the independence of the Lloyd's broker. As regards non-insurance interests all new holders of 20% or more of the capital are required to give a Letter of Undertaking.

Ultimate Net Loss
The loss to a reinsured after deduction is made for all recoveries and salvages.

"Umbrella" arrangements
An arrangement entered into between a Lloyd's broker and a non-Lloyd's broker not within the same group, whereby the Lloyd's broker permits certain employees of the non-Lloyd's broker to act on the Lloyd's broker's behalf (ie with the status and degree of responsibility equal to that of an authorised full-time employee of the Lloyd's broker) in the conduct of business with Lloyd's underwriters' such business being placed on the slips of, and for the account of, the Lloyd's broker.

Unearned premium
That part of the premium (if any) which relates to that part of a policy period which has yet to run.

Unconnected name
An underwriting member who is not subject to a vocational undertaking.

Underwriting agent
A registered underwriting agent is a firm or company permitted by the Council to act as an underwriting agent at Lloyd's. There are three different types of underwriting agent:
1) managing agent
2) members' agent
3) an agent which combines both functions (normally described as a managing agent).

Underwriting agency agreement
The contract or contracts entered into by an underwriting member with the underwriting agent or agents selected by him to underwrite a class or classes of insurance business at Lloyd's.

Utmost good faith (Uberrimae Fides)
A contract of insurance is a contract based upon the utmost good faith, and if the utmost good faith is breached by either party, the contract may be avoided by the other party.

Vocational Name
A member of Lloyd's who has signed an undertaking that he will remain in full-time employment with a Lloyd's underwriting agent or Lloyd's broker.

Void policy
One which in law does not exist.

Voidable policy
Where the underwriter or the insured had the right to avoid a policy (eg in event of a breach of utmost good faith) the policy is termed "voidable".

War and Civil War Exclusion Agreement
An undertaking between Lloyd's underwriters and many insurance companies generally not to accept war and civil war risks on property on land. (See Waterborne Agreement)

Warranty
It is defined as a "warranty by which the insured undertakes that some particular thing shall or shall not be done, or that some condition shall be fulfilled, or whether he affirms or negatives the existence of a particular state of facts." Non-compliance constitutes breach of warranty and the underwriter is discharged from liability as from the date of the breach.

Waterborne Agreement
A market understanding whereby underwriters only cover marine cargo against war risks whilst they are on the vessel. This rule is relaxed only in the case of goods in a transhipping port for a short period awaiting onward carriage.

Without prejudice
An agreement made by an insurer, without prejudicing his right to act differently on some future occasion.

Working member
a) A member of the Society who occupies himself principally with

the conduct of business at Lloyd's by a Lloyd's broker or underwriting agent;

b) A member of the Society who has gone into retirement but who immediately before his retirement so occupied himself.

Written line
The amount or percentage written on the broker's slip by an underwriter accepting a risk to indicate the maximum liability he is prepared to accept.

Year of Account
The year to which a risk is allocated and to which all premiums and claims in respect of that risk are attributed. The year of account of a risk is determined by the calendar year in which it is first signed at LPSO. A year of account is normally closed by reinsurance at the end of 36 months.

Chapter I

THE BASIC PURPOSE AND NATURE OF INSURANCE AND ITS VALUE TO THE COMMUNITY

THE WAY INSURANCE OPERATES

Insurance provides financial compensation for the effects of misfortune, the payments for claims being made from the accumulated contributions from the policyholders and held in underwriters' fund.

Insurance is thus a risk transfer mechanism and underwriters are the "risk takers".

There are two primary functions:–

A. A way of spreading losses among the many policy holders which would otherwise have to be met by persons or individual firms

FUND

Premiums from many policyholders

One claim from individual

Insurers should always have the latest available statistics to enable them to calculate the amount of premium required now for losses that may arise in the future.

An example of a calculation of the premium for property insurance

$$\frac{\text{Losses}}{\text{Values at risk}} \times \frac{100}{1} = \text{Rate per cent}$$

plus an additional percentage for expenses, commissions, and profits.

B. Assisting to alleviate worry for the insured by providing a form of security.

Examples of Provision of Security

To enable the repair or rebuilding of a house after a fire by paying a claim.

Whenever potential liability is involved security is important, and unless insured a motor car driver may have to pay out heavy compensation for another person's personal injuries if he was held responsible.

Risks that are not Insurable

These may be defined as those risks which are contrary to public interest, whether or not a specific exclusion is embodied in legislation, and war risks other than certain specific classes where the accumulation of values is considered manageable in relation to insurance funds. War risks cover may be given on ships, aircraft and on persons but motor cars are excluded.

Certain risks insurers normally choose not to insure

Risks arising through loss of market, bad marketing and economic conditions are not predictable and could be within the control of the person wishing to insure.

Secondary Functions are as follows:–

Industries avoid need to maintain funds to cover possible losses.

Security is provided to allow for the finance of overseas trade and granting of mortgages.

Investment by insurers of funds provide capital to industry and commerce.

Surveys and underwriting advice by insurers assist in prevention of loss, injury and fire waste.

Substantial contribution to invisible exports through overseas premiums.

REINSURANCE

Reinsurance is basically an extension of the concept of insurance, in that it passes on part of the risk for which an original insurer is liable. A contract of reinsurance is between the insurer and reinsurer only and legally there is no direct link between the original insured and any reinsurer.

Reasons for Reinsurance

Protection or cover against exceptionally large individual losses.

Example

A fire occurs in an oil refinery which has an insured value of £120 million and the total material damage losses are £20 million. An insurer has agreed to take 10% of the risk, thus he is liable for a loss of £2 million. The insurer may be able to recover part of this loss from a reinsurer if he has made suitable reinsurance arrangements, thus he is protected from a loss arising on one policy.

Example

An insurer receives claims under twenty separate policies covering various insured premises in Darwin. The total cost of a disaster to reinsurers is £120 million and the total of the claims on the one insurer is £4 million. Adequate reinsurance arrangements (catastrophe excess of loss) would protect him from an accumulation of losses arising from a number of policies.

Avoiding undue fluctuation in Underwriting results

The aim is to secure a balanced account and results each year without "peaks and troughs".

To obtain an international spread of risk

This is important when a country is vulnerable to natural disasters and an insurer is heavily committed in that country but perhaps not writing direct risks in others which do not have the same problems.

Example

An insurer writes a large account in the Carribean area which is prone to natural disasters thus he would be willing to reinsure business relating to risks in Europe.

To increase the capacity of the direct insurer

Many direct insuring companies reinsure with Lloyd's having accepted more of a risk than they are able to keep.

REVIEW OF MAIN CLASSES OF BUSINESS AT LLOYD'S

FIRE

The Lloyd's Fire Policy covers:–
1. Fire and/or lightning
2   (a) fire consequent upon explosion wherever explosion occurs.
    (b) explosion consequent upon fire on premises insured.
    (c) explosion of domestic boilers and/or gas used for domestic purposes or for heating and/or lighting.

Average is applied where there is underinsurance.
Additional Perils may be added at additional premium.
They may be classified as follows:–

Chemical Perils –	full explosion
Social Perils –	riot, civil commotion and malicious damage
Natural Perils –	storm, tempest, flood, earthquake
Miscellaneous Perils –	burst pipes and water damage, aircraft or other aerial devices or articles dropped therefrom, impact by vehicles, horses or cattle of third party, sprinkler leakage.

Business Interruption

The fire insurance policy covering material damage makes no provision for loss of earnings or additional expenses incurred in maintaining or re-establishing the business after damage.

A fire in business premises can cause serious interruption or dislocation to the business, resulting in diminution of trade during a period following the damage, and certain standing charges might still be required to be paid even though the business may be entirely stopped for a period.

The policy covers reduction in profit due to the reduction in the volume of trade as a result of the damage and increase in cost of working.

THEFT INSURANCE

Underwriters qualify Theft 1968 Act wording and define 'theft' within the following wording:–

Covers loss of or damage to property within the premises by theft or attempted theft.

Insurance does not cover loss or damage caused by theft or attempted theft:–

a) unless following

   i)   entry to or exit from the premises by forcible and violent means

   ii) assault, violence or threat thereof to the Assured, the Assured's employees or people to whom the Assured's property is entrusted.

b) of property by or in collusion with any of the Assured's employees or inmates of the Assured's Premises.

c) of property in any yard or open space.

MONEY

Covers transit risks, cash collections from customers or clients, other transits as specified, premises risks, and loss of stamps as defined. Subject to exclusions and conditions.

JEWELLERY, FURS AND PERSONAL EFFECTS

Covers loss or damage to property specified from whatsoever cause within geographical limits of G.B. N.I. Isle of Man, Channel Islands and Ireland, subject to exclusions.

HOUSEHOLDERS

Covers buildings and contents against a comprehensive list of perils including fire, additional perils, theft and public liability.

GOODS IN TRANSIT

All risks cover for property being loaded onto, carried on or unloaded from motor vehicles and trailers including temporary garaging during transit in G.B.

BANKERS BLANKET POLICY

All insurance needs of bank, commonly known as "bond".

Covers fidelity, premises cover, transit of cash and valuables by employees, forgery, counterfeit currency loss, damage to office and contents.

5

May extend to cover computer fraud, safe deposit box liability and kidnap and ransom.

BUILDERS AND CONTRACTORS

Covers physical damage and public liability for the construction and erection and maintenance period.

PERSONAL ACCIDENT

Normally the maximum capital sum for death with a variety of scale for permanent total disablement, the most serious of which might carry the capital sum and cover for temporary disablement on a weekly basis.

ACCIDENT AND ILLNESS POLICY

As for accident policy but in addition capital sums payable for permanent total loss of sight of both eyes, permanent total disablement by illness of any kind.

MOTOR INSURANCE

Underwriters insure the following classes of risk:–

Private cars used for private and business purposes (other than the carriage of passengers for hire or reward). Goods-carrying vehicles used solely for private purposes are usually rated as private cars.

Motorcycles

Commercial vehicles (including private cars carrying passengers for hire or reward).

(i)   Goods-carrying vehicles
(ii) Hire cars, taxis, coaches and buses
(iii) Agricultural and forestry vehicles
(iv) Miscellaneous vehicles usually known as "Special Types", e.g. ambulances, mobile plant and excavators, mobile shops, fork lift trucks, etc.

Motor Trade Risks covering vehicles used by motor traders. Motor trade risks may also cover the internal or premises risks of the motor trader.

The Comprehensive Policy covers:–

Loss of or damage to insured's vehicles and accessories and spare parts thereon by
   (i) fire and theft
  (ii) accidental damage
 (iii) malicious damage
 (iv) frost (except motor cycles)
Third party liabilities including passenger liability.
Liability of passengers ⎫
Personal accident benefits ⎪ In respect of
Loss of rugs, clothing and personal effects ⎬ private cars
Medical Expenses ⎪
Emergency treatment ⎭

May also extend to cover

Legal costs for manslaughter or reckless or dangerous driving causing death.
Breakage of windscreen and windows
Legal liability to paid driver for accident
Loss of use
Cost of delivery to insured in U.K. following accident
Foreign use
Fire damage to garage ⎫
Loss of Road Fund Licence ⎬ In respect of private cars.
Towing of Trailer or Caravan ⎭

PUBLIC LIABILITY (THIRD PARTY)

The cover provides:–
(1) An indemnity to the insured against liability at law for damages paid to claimants for bodily injury or disease (fatal or non-fatal) or damage to property
(2) Claimants' costs and expenses
(3) Insured's costs and expenses incurred with underwriters' written consent.

PROFESSIONAL INDEMNITY

Covers liability for professional negligence for a range of professional assureds.

PRODUCTS LIABILITY

Covers legal liability for bodily injury or property damage which arises out of goods or products (including food and drink) manufactured, constructed, altered, repaired, serviced, treated, sold supplied or distributed by insured.

EMPLOYER'S LIABILITY

Covers legal liability for damages if any person under contract of service or apprenticeship sustains bodily injury or disease or death resulting therefrom . . . arising out of and in course of employment by insured.

LIVESTOCK INSURANCE

This covers the insured against death of animals as a result of accident, illness or disease.

MARINE

Marine insurance is an insurance contract against losses incidental to a lawful "marine adventure". The Marine Insurance Act 1906 was an Act to codify the law to that date.

Insurable Interest

Anyone who has an insurable interest in a lawful marine adventure may insure e.g. shipowners, parties interested in monies (freight, passage money, profit etc.) where the insured property may be endangered by maritime perils, charterers, those exposed to liabilities to third parties which may arise by reason of maritime perils. Insurers may reinsure their interest. Master and crew have an insurable interest in their wages. The cost of insurance (premiums) may be insured. Cargo owners have an interest as do owners of property involved in the offshore oil and gas industry.

Period of Insurance

Ship and Freight—for time or voyage or 'mixed, i.e. time and voyage. Cargo—for voyage, and frequently warehouse to warehouse. Also cargo covers, for declaration purposes, of voyages which commence during a period of time stated in the cover. Cover usually limited to 60 days after discharge from vessel.

Coverage and Insured Perils

The standard MAR form is used for both hull and cargo risks, with appropriate clauses attached.

Clauses for Hull Insurance

The standard clauses show "named perils" covered by the policy and cover loss of or damage to the subject matter insured caused by:–

Perils of the seas rivers lakes or other navigable waters, fire, explosion, violent theft by persons from outside the vessel, jettison, piracy, breakdown or accident to nuclear installations or reactors, contact with aircraft or similar objects, or objects falling therefrom, land conveyance, dock or harbour equipment or installation, earthquake volcanic eruption or lightning.

additionally, the insurance covers:–

loss of or damage to the subject matter insured caused by accidents in loading discharging or shifting cargo or fuel, bursting of boilers breakage of shafts or any latent defect in the machinery or hull, negligence of Master Officers Crew or Pilots, negligence of repairers or charterers provided such repairers or charterers are not an Assured hereunder, barratry of Master Officers or Crew, provided such loss or damage has not resulted from want of due diligence by the Assured, Owners or Managers.

The policy extends to cover three quarters of the liability for damage caused to another vessel by collision and three quarters of the cost of defending any action or limiting liabilities.

The Policy is subject to a deductible.

Cargo Clauses

Two of the three sets cover named perils in that they name precisely what is covered and not covered. (Institute Cargo clauses B & C). The Institute Cargo clauses (C) provide the basic standard cover against major casualties.

The Institute Cargo Clauses (A) cover all risks of loss or damage due to a fortuity excluding loss or damage caused by stated exclusions.

Claims
Total Loss (including Constructive Total Loss) and Partial Loss

A loss may be either total or partial. Any loss other than a total loss, as hereinafter defined, is a partial loss.

A total loss may be either an actual total loss or a constructive total loss.

Actual total loss may occur where the subject matter insured is destroyed or so damaged as to cease to be a thing of the kind insured or where the insured is irretrievably deprived thereof.

The M.I.A. 1906 defines constructive total loss (C.T.L.) and states the right of the insured to claim as a partial loss, or abandon the subject matter insured to the insurer and claim for C.T.L. It also outlines the method of giving notice of abandonment; if the notice of abandonment is accepted the abandonment is irrevocable. In practice insurers generally decline the notice of abandonment, although, after payment of the claim they are entitled to take over the interest of the insured in what is left of the subject matter insured.

Partial Loss

(i) *General Average*

There is a general average act where any extraordinary sacrifice or expenditure is *voluntarily and reasonably* made or incurred in time of peril for the purpose of preserving the property imperilled in the common adventure and the whole of the property thereby preserved shall contribute to the loss sustained or expenditure incurred. General average arises irrespective of insurance and provided the general average contribution arises from a peril insured against a claim would be recoverable under the policy (under-insurance would reduce the claim).

(ii) *Particular Average*

Is a *partial* loss of, or damage to, the subject matter insured, caused by a peril insured against, which is not a general average loss.

Salvage Charges

Are the charges recoverable under maritime law by a salvor *independently of contract*, i.e. by a voluntary third party salvor

10

successfully saving maritime property in peril at sea. Provided the salvage arose from the operation of an insured peril, there would be a right of recovery under the insurance. (Any under-insurance would reduce the claim).

Duty of Insured (Sue and Labour)

Underwriters pay charges incurred by the insured in an effort to avert or minimise losses which would be recoverable under the insurance.

AVIATION

The Standard Aircraft Policy cover is as follows:–
Section 1. Loss or Damage to Aircraft
      2. Legal Liability to Third Parties other than Passengers
      3. Legal Liability to Passengers

Section 1

Pay for, replace or repair accidental loss or damage to aircraft arising from risks covered including disappearance if unreported 60 days after commencement of flight. If insured for risks of flight— pay reasonable emergency expenses up to 10%.
But excluding:–
   Wear and tear and breakdown
   Damage which has progressive or cumulative effect

Section 2

Legal liability and agreed law costs for bodily injury or damage to property
Subject limits each person and each accident.

Section 3

Legal liability and agreed costs in respect of claims from passengers for injury or damage to, or loss of personal effects and baggage
Subject to limits each passenger and each aircraft.

Other Types of Cover include:–

Products Legal Liability
   Cover legal liability of manufacturers or repairer.

11

Airport Liability Policy
Covers legal liability of airport operator for claims for bodily injury or damage.

Loss of Licence Insurance
Covers aircrew who lose licences in event of being unfit through accident or illness.

Personal Accident
Effected by passengers or aircrew for own benefit.
Group Policies on declaration basies.
Automatic P.A. cover may be provided by firms for their passengers.

Cargo
All risks cover for whole of transit.

Loss of Use
Cover for loss of earnings following aircraft being laid-up for repairs.

REINSURANCE

The main methods of reinsurance are as follows:–

Facultative

This is the oldest method. Individual risks are submitted to the reinsurers who may accept or decline as they think fit.

Treaty

This is the method predominantly used. It is automatic and, briefly, is an arrangement entered into between one insurer (the ceding insurer) and a number of other insurers (the reinsurers) who agree to accept, automatically any reinsurances (cessions) falling within the terms of the treaty.

The main types of reinsurance are as follows:–

Proportional Reinsurance

Quota Share Treaty—The insurer agrees to pass on to the reinsurer a fixed proportion of all their acceptances (usually subject to a fixed upper limit) of business within the scope of the treaty.

Example
Fire and Allied Lines Business.

75% Quota Share up to a maximum of 75% of £1,000,000 any one risk. The reinsurer accepts 75% of all risks, and receives 75% of the premium, but only to a maximum amount of £750,000 (being 75% of £1,000,000). The ceding insurer must make separate arrangements if the risk is over £1 million.

Surplus Treaty—The insurer agrees to pass on only the difference between the amount he has accepted and the amount he wishes to keep (retention) subject to a fixed upper limit.

Surplus treaties are arranged in lines, based on the insurer's retention.

Example

An insurer effects a ten-line treaty with other insurers. This means that for every line he retains for his own account he can reinsure up to ten such lines, or, in other words, reinsurers automatically accept up to ten times his retention, e.g.

Retention	Acceptance	Reinsurance
£5,000	£55,000	£50,000

These figures are based on a ten-line treaty. If it is necessary to accept more than £55,000, £50,000 only can be placed with the treaty and facultative cover must be sought for the balance, unless there is a second surplus treaty which will allow for further reinsurance.

Facultative-obligatory reinsurance falls between facultative and treaty: whereas the ceding insurer can choose whether or not to cede to the reinsurer any risks falling within the terms of the agreement, the reinsurer is bound to accept automatically the business offered. Thus it is essentially a surplus treaty between two contracting parties.

Non-Proportional Reinsurance

Excess of Loss— The insurer decides the amount that he is prepared to bear on each and every loss, and arranges reinsurance to relieve him of any liability in excess of that amount.

13

The main attraction of excess of loss reinsurance is the protection that this can provide against catastrophe losses involving accumulations of net retentions (known as Catastrophe Excess of Loss Reinsurance). Another use for excess of loss reinsurance is to protect the reinsured for a loss involving only one risk (known as Risk Excess of Loss Reinsurance). This can in some cases take the place of pro-rata reinsurance treaties, either because such cover would be unsuitable or impossible. For example where original policies provide unlimited indemnity as for employers liability or motor business. This class of reinsurance is usually arranged in layers often with a high underlying excess.

Catastrophe excess of loss reinsurance is essential where original coverage is granted for natural perils such as wind, storm, tempest, hurricane, earthquake, bush fires etc in order to prevent too great an exposure to any one event/disaster.

Example

To pay up to £300,000 ultimate nett loss each and every loss excess of £100,000 ultimate nett loss each and every loss. Thus the reinsurer's liability is £300,000 after the reinsured has paid a loss of £100,000 after claiming on any other reinsurance proportional treaty he may have (ultimate nett loss).

Stop Loss Reinsurance or Excess of Loss Ratio

By means of surplus or normal risk excess of loss reinsurance the reinsured can reduce its net liability on individual risks to a figure well within its compass, yet by reason of the incidence of losses it may well find itself with a high claims ratio at the end of the year. Stop loss reinsurance is the form of protection which in those circumstances makes it possible to limit such loss ratio to an agreed percentage of the original insured's premium income on business protected.

Personal stop loss reinsurances are also used by individual Members to obtain protection against an overall underwriting loss on any one year of account. However the member will have to carry some loss.

REVISION NOTES

INSURANCE

There are two primary functions, that of spreading losses and that of providing security.

Risks that are not Insurable

Those risks which are contrary to public interest, whether or not a specific exclusion is embodied in legislation.
   War risk cover other than specific classes.

Certain risk insurers normally choose not to insure

Risks arising through loss of market, bad marketing and economic conditions are not measurable and could be within the control of the person wishing to insure.

The main classes of business at Lloyd's are:—

Non-marine:– Fire, Theft, Money, Jewellery, Furs and Personal Effects, Householders, Goods in Transit, Bankers Blanket Bond, Builders and Contractors, Personal Accident (and Illness), Public Liability (Third Party), Professional Indemnity, Products Liability, Employers Liability, Livestock.

Marine:– Hull, Cargo and Freight and Offshore Oil and Gas Industry.

Aviation:– Hull and Third Party and Passenger Liability, also Airport Liability, Loss of Licence, Cargo and Loss of Use.

Motor:– Private Cars, Commercial Vehicles, Motor Cycles and Motor Trade Risks.

Reasons for Reinsurance

Protection or cover against exceptionally large individual losses.
Avoiding undue fluctuations in underwriting results.
To obtain an international spread of risk.
To increase capacity of the direct insurer.

Facultative

Individual risks are submitted to the reinsurers who may accept or decline as they think fit.

Treaty

An arrangement entered into between one insurer and a number of other insurers who agree to accept automatically any reinsurances falling within the terms of the treaty.

Proportional
Quota Share Treaty.
Surplus.

Non-Proportional

Excess of loss—catastrophe or risk.
Stop loss or excess of loss ratio.

MENTAL REVISION QUESTIONS

1. What is the primary function of insurance?
2. How do insurers endeavour to charge fair premiums for differing risks?
3. What risks are not insurable?
4. Which risks do insurers normally choose not to insure?
5. Which perils may be added to the Lloyd's Fire Policy?
6. How are the main classes of risk in motor insurance split?
7. What are the usual benefits under a personal accident policy?
8. What risks can be insured by a marine policy other than the hull of a ship?
9. What forms can liability insurance take?
10. Which set of Institute Cargo Clauses give the widest cover?

Chapter II

LEGAL PRINCIPLES GOVERNING INSURANCE TRANSACTIONS

(i) UTMOST GOOD FAITH AND ITS SIGNIFICANCE IN THE RELATIONSHIP BETWEEN UNDERWRITERS AND BROKERS.

Insurance contracts differ from commercial contracts because the proposer is the only person who knows all about the risk he wishes to insure and his own past insurance history.

Insurers have to rely on the information supplied by the proposer in their consideration of any risk.

Insurers may ask questions as in a proposal form which the proposer must answer in full and truthfully although for consumer insurances insurers generally reduce this duty to the best of the proposer's knowledge and belief. In certain cases their representatives may survey a risk. It is therefore necessary to have a principle which allows insurers to come off risk or refuse payment of a claim when an insurance has been obtained by telling untruths or hiding facts. There is a general duty of disclosure on the proposer in addition to answers given to any questions on the proposed form.

Similarly insurers must state the terms of the insurance clearly during negotiations.

The rule of utmost good faith applies in insurance contracts and is a common law duty.

A duty is on the insured to state facts relating to a risk accurately, these are termed "material facts" and are those which would affect the acceptance or rating of a risk.

Insurers are not interested in matters of opinion, only fact.

This duty applies:–

— Throughout negotiation of a risk
— To any alteration in the risk whilst that alteration is being negotiated with the insurers
— To any renewal of the insurance

Examples of Facts which Matter

The refusal of another insurer to renew an insurance policy of the type being negotiated. A firm omitting to state that one of the partners of the firm has been refused theft insurance whilst trading alone in the same goods on the same premises.

A bungalow has a thatched roof and not one of slates or tiles and therefore presents an increased fire risk.

Alteration during policy period

A policy condition may require the insured to advise insurers of any increase or alteration in risk during the policy period.

Disclosure by Broker

The broker is the agent for the insured and his responsibility is to his principal and jointly to see that insurers are fully informed of all material facts necessary to underwrite the risk.

Representations

These are factual statements made verbally or in writing by the proposer or his brokers which relate to the risk to be insured. They must be substantially true if they relate to matters of fact and if they are not, insurers may refuse to pay a subsequent claim.

Example

"No claim over the past fifteen years on a household policy". (A claim was made five years prior to statement).

Remedies of Insurers

If the insured is in breach of utmost good faith the policy may be of no effect from the time of the breach or insurers may refuse to pay a claim. Insurers may overlook the breach when they do not consider it to affect the risk or claim.

In the case of fraud however the policy has no legal validity.

Contractual Duty

For consumer insurances the Proposal Form generally contains declaration to be signed stating that to the best of insured's

18

knowledge and belief that information is true and agreeing that proposal form is basis of and incorporated in policy.

(ii) BASIC ESSENTIAL PRINCIPLES UNDERLYING EVERY CONTRACT OF INSURANCE INCLUDING THE PURPOSE AND EFFECTS OF WARRANTIES

LAW OF CONTRACT

A contract is a legally binding agreement between two or more parties and the policy of insurance is the evidence of the contract.

Contracts may be simple or speciality contracts (or deeds). The great majority of insurance contracts are simple contracts.

There is no necessity for simple contracts to be in writing, however in practice insurance contracts are evidenced in writing and S.22 of the Marine Insurance Act, 1906 requires marine insurance contracts to be in writing.

To constitute a valid contract the parties to it must have intended their agreement to give rise to legal obligations.

Essential Elements of Simple Contracts

There are seven essential elements of simple contracts and these are:–

1. *Capacity*. Both parties must be capable of entering into a legally enforceable agreement, however some classes of person have limited capacity to contract in law.

   These include minors who can only enter into binding contracts for necessaries or for their own benefit. (Insurance contracts are considered for their own benefit).

   Common Law Corporations who have unlimited contractual powers.

   Statutory Corporations where the contract must be in accordance with the object for which corporation was created else it is ultra vires and void.

2. *Legality*. The parties must intend to enter into a legal relation-

19

ship. The subject – matter of the contract must not be contrary to law (for instance a marine cargo policy with an enemy national in time of war).

3. *Possibility*. Performance of the contract must be possible in fact and in law.

4. *Offer*. There must be an unrevoked offer by one party to another or others.

   The offer may be written, verbal or by conduct and it must be communicated.

   The offer is usually made by proposer and contained in a duly completed proposal form completed by the prospective insured or is contained in the written details on the slip shown to underwriters. The issue of a proposal form by insurers does not itself constitute an offer. It is simply an invitation to a prospective insured to offer an insurance which the insurer may accept or reject or agree to accept on certain terms only.

5. *Acceptance*. The acceptance must be unqualified and must coincide exactly with the offer.

   It may be written, verbal or by conduct and must generally be communicated, and it is open only to person to whom offer was made.

   If the insurers impose higher rates than normal or more stringent terms after an offer by the proposer it becomes a counter offer which proposer may accept or reject.

6. *Consensus Ad Idem*. Unrevoked offer and unqualified acceptance are required.

   There must be complete agreement between the parties (a party may escape liability by showing they were mistaken as to what has apparently been agreed, but mistake of law will not avoid the contract).

7. *Consideration*. Where a person wishes to enforce a promise made to them by another they must show that they gave something to, or did something for, that other in return for the promise e.g. the premium is the consideration.

The consideration must "move" from promisee to promisor, it need not be adequate but must be of some value and genuine.

Consideration from the insured to the insurer—this is the premium.

Consideration from the insurer to the insured—this is the promise to compensate the insured or to make certain payments in the event of certain events taking place. This promise is applicable whether a claim arises during the period of the insurance or not.

Validity of Contracts

Void. Contracts which are contrary to statute or public policy, or which are induced by fraud or when an essential element is missing.

Voidable. When it is open to one of the parties to avoid the contract if they choose.

Unenforceable. Contracts which fail because of some evidential defect e.g. a marine insurance contract which has not been evidenced in writing.

Termination of Contract

A contract may be terminated in the following ways:–

Performance by all parties.
By Agreement between parties.
Through Subsequent Impossibility (frustration)—the contract cannot be performed because after the time when the contract was made and prior to completion, an event occurs which destroys the basis of the contract but without the fault of either party.

Breach of Contract is a failure to carry out obligations which does not terminate the contract but gives the other party a right of action for breach e.g. failure of insurers to pay a claim.

Remedies for Breach of Contract

At common law damages may be awarded which may be liquidated or unliquidated (the amount may be stated in the contract or not).

The courts can also order specific performance (the contract

21

must be performed) or an injunction (which is an order preventing an act).

Construction

The contract is construed according to ordinary language except where terms are defined in a contract (e.g. Aviation and Personal Accident policies.)

The conditions of a contract are binding if agreed prior to completion.

WARRANTIES

Underwriters may include into an insurance policy a stipulation which should be complied with by the insured. These are termed 'warranties' and are used to control the nature of a risk.

A warranty is an undertaking as to fact or performance concerning the risk written into an insurance policy and may need to be complied with strictly and literally.

Non-compliance constitutes breach of warranty and the underwriter is discharged from liability as from the date of breach. However, the Statement of Insurance Practice, which does not apply to marine and aviation risks and only applies to policyholders resident in the UK and insured in their private capacity states that underwriters will not repudiate liability to indemnify a policyholder on the grounds of a breach of warranty or condition where the circumstances of the loss are unconnected with the breach unless fraud is involved.

The Statement has been voluntarily adopted by underwriters.

Examples of Warranties are:–

Fire Insurance	That all oily or greasy rags be placed in metal receptacles and removed from the building daily
	That not more than 200 gallons of paraffin to be kept in an ironmonger's premises at any one time
Burglary	That premises are not unoccupied at night
Insurance	That certain types of approved locks are fitted
Marine Insurance	That goods are packed in tin-lined cases.

Non-compliance with a warranty may be excused by insurers if

they are notified and an additional premium paid if required.
Implied warranties. These are found only in marine insurance.
They are warranties which are automatically applicable, although
they do not appear in the policy document. An example is the
warranty that a vessel is seaworthy.

INSURABLE INTEREST

An insured can only take out an insurance policy if the happening of
an insured event will cause him or his dependants financial or
personal loss.

This is termed "insurable interest" and is the legal right to insure,
without which no insurance contract can be enforced in a Court.

Without the need for insurable interest people could enter into
gambling or wagering contracts which would be to the detriment of
the other policy-holders and the public as a whole.

Examples

Mr Smith cannot insure Mr Green's house because if the house is
destroyed or damaged by fire Mr Smith will suffer no financial
loss.

Mr Smith cannot insure Mr Green's legal liability for accidents
sustained by Mr Green's workmen, for if one of Mr Green's
workmen should claim against his employer, Mr Green, then Mr
Smith would not be financially concerned.

A person may insure where they will be financially prejudiced by
loss or damage to property or may incur legal liability arising from
such property or from their own actions.

Examples of person who may insure

Owners or joint owners of property with the permission of the
other joint owner—joint owner can insure for the whole value of
the property on behalf of the other.

A person who has lawful possession of goods of another—a dry
cleaner, garage proprietor or hotel keeper.

Those who have property within their care—an executor after
someone's death.

Agents—insurance brokers insuring on behalf of their clients.

An underwriter—may insure a risk he has underwritten (reinsurance).

Mortgagees—Building Societies may insure to the value of their loan.

Insurable interest must exist both when the insurance is taken out and at the time of a claim for non-marine policies and at time of claim for marine policies.

A non-marine policy cannot be transferred or assigned to a third party without consent because the policy is regarded as a "personal" contract between the underwriters and the insured and rated partly on the record of the insured.

INDEMNITY

The object of an insurance policy is to place the insured in the same financial position as he was prior to any loss occurring.

This principle applies to all insurance contracts, except those on life and of personal accident insurance where difficulties arise in placing values on life and limb.

Example

If a carpet was destroyed by a fire and at the time of the fire it was nearly worn out it would be contrary to the principle of indemnity (and fairness to the other policyholders) to pay the price of a new carpet. Otherwise the insured would be tempted to destroy his own property. The insurers pay in this case the current price of a new carpet but reduce the payment made to allow for the age and condition of the existing carpet.

Many household and commercial policies agree to replace items insured by new items provided the insured uses the value of new items in his calculations of the sum insured.

Indemnity may be provided for example by:-

Cash payment

Reinstatement—cost of rebuilding of a house paid by the insurers (this is rarely done due to the problems involved)

Repair—repairs are authorised to a damaged motor vehicle and insurers pay the garage account.

24

Replacement—when an aircraft is lost, insurers may replace it with an aircraft of similar age and type.

Variations to Indemnity are as follows:–

Where the insured and insurer agree in advance the amount to be paid in the event of total loss of property this is termed a "valued policy".

Where the insured bears part of the loss termed "an excess" he will not be fully indemnified but may gain a reduction in premium for bearing an excess unless this has been imposed by the insurer.

When the insured is under-insured he will not fully recover the sum insured in the event of a total loss and insurers may reduce partial losses payments by applying "average" where the insured is compelled to bear part of the loss himself.

PROXIMATE CAUSE

There is a valid claim under a policy of insurance only if the loss, damage or liability is arising from an insured peril. Thus when a claim occurs the cause of the loss must be established to decide whether or not it is within the cover of the policy.

At law only the dominant and effective cause of the loss is considered. Any other remote causes are disregarded.

The cause of a loss may be an insured peril specifically mentioned in the policy or a peril specifically excluded by the policy or a cause which the policy does not mention.

The law states that the sequence of events leading from the insured peril to the actual loss must be unbroken for the loss to be payable under the policy.

Thus circumstances can arise when an excluded peril is the genuine cause of the loss and insurers are not therefore liable for the loss.

Examples

A single cause which is insured peril i.e. fire under fire policy— liability.

An excluded cause followed by insured peril if no break e.g. riot causing a fire—no liability.

The onus of proof that a loss is caused by an insured peril rests upon the claimant.

25

The courts and insurers always consider the dominant cause of a loss which need not necessarily be the cause nearest in point of time.

Example

If a vessel is torpedoed and damaged but sinks during a subsequent storm, insurers will not consider that the storm caused the sinking (although nearest in point of time) but that the torpedo was the real cause of the loss.

The principle operates to benefit both insured and insurer as follows:–

The insurer is secure from claims for losses remotely caused by a peril insured against but effectively caused by a peril outside the scope of the policy.

The insured is protected against non payment of a reasonable claim although a remote cause is not a peril insured against.

SUBROGATION

Applicable *only* to contracts of indemnity. Once insurers have fully met the claim made, they are entitled under common law to take over all the legal rights of their insured so that the insurers' loss is cut down or fully recoverable.

Examples

When an insured is involved in a motor accident caused by the negligence of another driver insurers can seek to recover the damage to the insured vehicle from the other driver.

Under the terms of a contract whereby a warehouseman is liable to pay part of any loss to the insured if the insured's goods are destroyed or damaged while in the warehouseman's possession.

After paying for a total loss of property insurers may be entitled to the salvage remaining i.e. the wreck of a car or damaged toys after a fire in a toy shop.

In practice insurers can modify the common law position:–

A policy condition in non-marine policies usually enables insurers to exercise their right of subrogation before payment of any claim is made to the insured by the insurers.

Where legal liability is concerned insurers often defend actions in court on behalf of their insured.

Agreements, commonly called "knock for knock", between insurers not to pursue rights of subrogation in motor insurance. Each insurer paying for damage to the particular car he has insured.

If an insured claims for damage to his vehicle from his insurers but also receives a payment from another motorist involved in the accident he is expected to hold this payment in trust for insurers if he has already received payment from them.

CONTRIBUTION

An insured may have more than one policy covering the same risk against the same peril. This may arise inadvertently where an agent also insures property as well as a principal or deliberately where an insured doubts the security or cover of one policy.

Under the rules of indemnity the insured is not allowed to claim more than the true amount of his loss. He should not claim the full loss from one insurer and a similar amount from other insurers.

The principle allows the insured to claim the full loss from one insurer who then has the right to ask the other insurers who are also liable to share the claims payment.

At common law rights arise after a loss has been paid to the insured and insurers then have to share the loss between themselves.

Modification by a Policy Condition

Most non-marine policies contain a clause limiting insurers' liability to their share of the loss when other policies also exist, thus the insured is obliged to claim proportionately from each insurer.

Example for Property Insurance

$$\frac{\text{Sum insured by individual insurer} \times \text{Loss}}{\text{Total sum insured}}$$

Some policies contain a clause which states that the loss will not be shared if the property is listed separately in another policy. This is termed the "Non Contribution Clause".

Example

The householders policy on contents would not cover specified items of jewellery insured under Jewellery, Furs and Personal Effects Policy.

III) THE DUTIES AND RESPONSIBILITIES OF A BROKER AND THE SIMPLE BASIS OF THE LAW OF AGENCY.

BROKERS

Functions of a Broker

To act as an intermediary.
To be a professional adviser.
To represent his client's interests.

Agency

In the ordinary sense of the word, an agent is a person who is employed to do something in the place of another.

The Lloyd's broker

Lloyd's brokers are committed to additional responsibilities on behalf of Lloyd's underwriters beyond normal insurance-broking practice and within the general law of agency.

Such resonsibilities include the preparation of policies which are submitted to Lloyd's Policy Signing Office for checking and signature on behalf of underwriters. Accounting between Lloyd's brokers and underwriters is transacted under the central accounting scheme which inevitably necessitates the application of procedures which vary the brokers' position in law by comparison with their dealings with insurance companies.

While therefore Lloyd's brokers in their company business would look to the general law of agency for an understanding of their status, within Lloyd's there are additional factors deriving from their relationships with Lloyd's underwriters and Lloyd's practices.

Appointment and termination of 'agency'

Insurance brokers are the agent of the insured, although in practice or by custom they may accept such appointments or responsibilities from others also.

The appointment of an agent may be:

(a) by an agreement in writing (i.e. by express agreement):

(b) by implication or conduct or by the situation of the parties:

(c) by necessity;

(d) by imposition.

Agents may in turn be:

(a) special (for a specific act only);

(b) general (empowered to do anything within certain limits);

(c) universal (unlimited powers).

In practical terms this means the following:

(a) By express agreement. Either verbally or in writing a specific appointment will be made which may contain conditions, e.g. a letter of appointment by a client or an insurance company's agency agreement.

(b) By implication or conduct. Someone may permit another to obtain or do things for him and commonly approve of what is done: e.g. a client may accept renewals automatically made on his behalf.

(c) By necessity. It may be impossible to get a principal's instructions, and a necessity arises forcing an agent to deal with the events.

If an agent does not have authority to contract for his principal or has exceeded his powers, then there is no binding contract.

It may be possible for the agent to obtain ratification of his acts without authority later, but if this is not possible a personal responsibility may well remain in the absence of some defence being available.

Should it be wished to terminate the relationship between a principal and an agent this may be accomplished by mutual agreement, revocation or operation of the law.

A mutual agreement to end a relationship should nevertheless deal with all aspects of the severance. There is no set procedure, but an exchange of letters or a record of conversations is important to avoid future liabilities being imposed on the agent. This record of events should indicate the date of termination, how the disposal of information and documents will be carried out, what responsibilities remain and how unpaid debts will be met.

Operation of the law may terminate agency relationships where:
   (a) the period of appointment has expired:
   (b) a particular transaction for which the agent was appointed
       has been completed or an agreed event has taken place;
   (c) the agency has become unlawful;
   (d) there has been death or insanity;
   (e) there has been bankruptcy or liquidation.

Insurance Brokers

The EEC Intermediaries Directive (1976) defines an insurance
broker as follows:–
   "Professional activities of persons who, acting with complete
   freedom as to their choice of undertaking, bring together, with a
   view to the insurance or reinsurance of risks, persons seeking
   insurance or reinsurance and insurance or reinsurance undertak-
   ings, carry out work preparatory to the conclusion of contracts of
   insurance or reinsurance and, where appropriate, assist in the
   administration and performance of such contracts, in particular
   in the event of a claim".
The prime difference between "insurance agents" and "insurance
brokers" is that an agent answers directly to the insurer; the
insurance broker relates to the policyholder. To this extent
therefore the term "agent" has come to have a special meaning
beyond the simple "agent" dealt with in the law of agency.

Agency Agreements

Agency agreements are required by many Lloyd's brokers before
they will undertake to accept business from non-Lloyd's brokers for
placement with Lloyd's. This is particularly so for motor business,
where, unusually, direct contact between the Lloyd's underwriters
and non-Lloyd's brokers does exist.
   Special requirements of the Committee of Lloyd's also exist for
this "direct motor" business.

Duties of a Broker

The general law of agency requires that an insurance broker
assumes responsibilities which require him:
   (a) to exercise due diligence in carrying out instructions within
       the responsibilities which he has undertaken;

(b) to exercise any skill he professes to have;
(c) to ensure the principal is aware of factors likely to affect his judgment in fulfilment of the contract;
(d) to render an account and not make any secret commission or profit beyond normal remuneration;
(e) to maintain confidentiality;
(f) not to delegate authority without specific permission.

The insurance broker and responsibility for negligence

An insurance broker like any other professional is legally responsible to his principal or other in the event he fails to use reasonable care.

The duties of care exercised are high and this was emphasised in 1963 when in Hedley Byrne v. Heller it was held that care on advice given had to be exercised by persons even without any formal contract. An insurance broker must be certain of the advice he gives in addition to carrying out specific and required acts on behalf of his principal.

Rights of An Insurance Broker

The insurance broker has a right of support from his principal in carrying out his responsibilities as agent of the insured. It is the duty of the principal to indemnify his agent for acts lawfully done and liabilities incurred in the carrying out of the responsibilities involved.

The right to the commission earned is fundamental and the fact that physically the commission is paid by the insurer by deduction does not make the broker into the agent of the insurer.

Broker's responsibility for Payment of Premium

In connection with the transaction of business involving Lloyd's Underwriters, it is the long standing custom that a Lloyd's broker is liable to the underwriters for the premium. So far as marine insurance is concerned this custom has been embodied in the Marine Insurance Act 1906 s.53 (i), it must be emphasised that the practice applies to all business placed at Lloyd's, not only marine.

31

Utmost Good Faith

The broker is the agent for the insured and not only must he disclose what has been communicated to him by his principal, but he must also disclose any circumstance of which he himself (though not the principal) may have knowledge.

Broker's responsibility to his client

A Broker's first responsibility is to his client. He will interpret his client's wishes and, when necessary, clarify these, resulting in a proposal from the client which will translate into an offer to an Underwriter.

At all times he will advance his client's interests and obtain the best possible terms and conditions. He will also endeavour to achieve the lowest possible premium commensurate with the security of the market he approaches.

On completion of placing the risk, the Broker will advise his client and produce a cover note confirming the agreed terms and conditions and setting out the security i.e. the list of Underwriters subscribing to the risk.

The Broker thereafter will give the client the service he can reasonably expect, with particular reference to the accounting of monies, both premiums and claims.

Broker's responsibility to the Underwriter

A Broker's responsibility to the Underwriter is essentially a Duty of Care—that is to say that any undertaking given to the Underwriter must be honoured and no material information withheld.

Whilst the Broker must portray the client's proposal in the most favourable light, this must not be at the expense of an honest presentation or, at worst, result in a mischievous or even fraudulent misrepresentation.

The Broker must therefore present to the Underwriter all the information at his disposal which is needed by the Underwriter to make a fair and reasonable appreciation of the risk being offered.

After the risk has been placed and any short-signing commitment has been honoured, the Broker will continue to have a responsibility to the Underwriter as far as monetary transactions are concerned.

32

The Broker will pay the premiums (which he has collected from his client) to the Underwriters within a reasonable time and within the period laid down at the time of placing the risk.

Should claims become payable, the details must be shown by the Broker to the Underwriter in an honest way as advised by the client and the monies, once collected, transmitted promptly to the client to avoid any further distress being suffered by the claimant and to put the insurer in a favourable light in the eye of the assured.

REVISION NOTES

UTMOST GOOD FAITH

This principle allows insurers to come off risk or refuse payment of a claim when an insurance has been obtained by telling untruths or hiding facts.

A duty is on the insured to state facts relating to a risk accurately, these are termed "material facts" and are those which would affect the acceptance or rating of a risk.

The broker is the agent for the insured and not only must he disclose what has been communicated to him by his principal, but he must also disclose any circumstance of which he himself (though not the principal) may have knowledge.

Representations are factual statements made verbally or in writing by the proposer or his brokers which relate to the risk to be insured. They must be substantially true if they relate to facts and if they are not, insurers may refuse to pay a subsequent claim.

Contract Law

The seven essential elements are capacity, offer, legality, possibility, acceptance, consensus ad idem and consideration. (C.O.L.-P.A.C.C.)

Validity

Void — Contracts which are contrary to statute or public policy, or which are induced by fraud or when an essential element is missing.

Voidable — When it is open to one of the parties to avoid the contract if they choose.

Unenforceable—Contracts which fail because of some evidential defect.

Warranties

Underwriters may include into an insurance policy a stipulation which must be complied with by the insured. These are termed "warranties" and are used to control the nature of a risk.

A warranty is an undertaking as to fact or performance concerning the risk written into an insurance policy and may need to be complied with strictly and literally.

Insurable Interest

An insured can only take out an insurance policy if the happening of an insured event will cause him or his dependants financial or personal loss.

This is termed "insurable interest" and is the legal right to insure, without which no insurance contract can be enforced in a Court.

Indemnity

The object of an insurance policy is to place the insured in the same financial position as he was prior to any loss occurring.

This principle applies to all insurance contracts, except those on life and of personal accident insurance where difficulties arise in placing values on life and limb.

Proximate Cause

There is a valid claim under a policy of insurance only if the loss, damage or liability is caused by an insured peril. Thus when a claim occurs the cause of the loss must be established to decide whether or not it is within the cover of the policy.

At law only the dominant and effective cause of the loss is considered. Any other remote causes are disregarded.

Subrogation

Applicable *only* to contracts of indemnity. Once insurers have fully met the claim made, they are entitled under common law to take over all the legal rights of their insured so that the insurers' loss is cut down or fully recoverable.

Contribution

The principle allows the insured to claim the full loss from one insurer who then has the right to ask the other insurers who are also liable to share the claims payment.

Most non-marine policies contain a clause limiting insurers' liability to their share of the loss when other policies also exist, thus the insured is obliged to claim proportionately from each insurer.

Brokers

Full-time specialists of professional standing. Lloyd's Bokers have paid necessary subscription and complied with other regulations to enable them to place business at Lloyd's.

For most purposes legally the agent of the policyholder and owes legal duty to him to protect client's interests.

May be sued for professional negligence, and must follow client's instructions.

Subject to common law of agency which requires Broker shall have technical knowledge of customs of business.

MENTAL REVISION QUESTIONS

1. What is a material fact?
2. What is a representation?
3. Name the seven essential elements of a simple contract.
4. What is meant by a voidable contract?
5. What is a warranty?
6. Which principle governs the legal right to insure?
7. What does the term "indemnity" mean?
8. Why is the principle of proximate cause of importance to underwriters?
9. Given an example of when subrogation might arise.
10. What are the main functions of a broker?

Chapter III

THE STRUCTURE OF THE LLOYD'S MARKET

i) THE NATURE OF LLOYD'S, THAT IS A SOCIETY OF INDIVIDUAL MEMBERS OPERATING IN A MARKET PLACE AND REGULATED BY A COUNCIL.

HISTORY OF LLOYD's

1688	*First known reference to Lloyd's Coffee House in Tower Street.*
1696	*Lloyd's News first published*—published three times a week but discontinued 23.2.1697.
1701	*Earliest surviving Shipping List*—these were forerunners of Lloyd's List.
1720	*Royal Charter created monopoly*—but underwriting by private individuals not prohibited (Repealed 1824).
1769	*Gambling element.* *New Lloyd's formed* by professional underwriters in Pope's Head Alley.
1771	*79 underwriters and brokers each subscribed £100 for removal to larger premises.* *First Committee of Lloyd's elected*—9 subscribers.
1774	*Rental of Rooms in Royal Exchange.* *Entry restricted to subscribers and connections.*
1796	*Resolved by Committee to Present Annual Reports and Accounts.*
1804	*Appointment of first Secretary of Lloyd's.*
1811	*Trust Deed signed by subscribers.* *Appointment of first Lloyd's Agencies.* *Admission more strictly regulated.* *Committee increased to 12.*
1837	*Lloyd's List daily.*
1857	*First deposit made with Committee by Underwriting Member.*

1871	*Lloyd's incorporated by Act of Parliament.*
1871–90	*Signal stations and telegraphic communications set-up. Lloyd's Act made Lloyd's a legal entity.*
1873	*Lloyd's Seal affixed to every Lloyd's policy.*
1898	*Heath wrote first reinsurance policy on American risks for English Company doing business in U.S.A.*
1903	*First non-marine deposit accepted.*
1906	*San Francisco Earthquake claims met.*
1907	*Excess of Loss reinsurance introduced by Heath.*
1908	*Annual audit introduced voluntarily. Premium Trust Fund introduced.*
1909–46	*Assurance Companies Acts made Audit and Premium Trust Fund compulsory.*
1911	*First aviation risk ever written.*
1916	*L.P.S.O. set-up.*
1937	*Additional Securities Ltd. formed to meet U.S. State Legislation requirements.*
1939	*American Trust Fund* for U.S. Dollar premiums.
1958	*Move to new building April 8.*
1968	*Nationals of countries outside British Commonwealth admitted to Membership.*
1969	*Women domiciled in U.K. may become members.*
1970	*Women of any nationality may be admitted as members.*
1974	*Women admitted to Room.*
1978	Extraordinary general meeting of members accepts recommendation to redevelop Lloyd's 1928 building.
1978	*Fisher Working Party constituted.*
1980	*Fisher Working Party Report published.* New Lloyd's Bill drafted based on Fisher proposals. AGM of Lloyd's members at Royal Albert Hall (first held outside Lloyd's since 1838 Royal Exchange Fire) approves draft Bill by majority of 99.6%.
1981	*First reading of Lloyd's Bill on January 22.* Second reading March 24. Parliamentary Committee demands "divestment" and "divorce". Lloyd's membership votes in favour of divestment, and against divorce. Bill held over.
1981	*Work begins on new building.* HM Queen Elizabeth The Queen Mother inaugurates construction on November 5.
1982	*Bill receives Third Reading in the House of Commons, March 9.* Third Reading Debate in House of Lords July 16.

Bill returns to House of Commons July 21. Royal Assent received, Bill becomes Lloyd's Act 1982, July 23. Election of first Council of Lloyd's in November. Appointment of three nominated members in December.

1983 First meeting of council of Lloyd's appoints first Chief Executive in January. Lloyd's appeal tribunal and disciplinary committees set up in February.

1984 Proposed requirements for divestment outlined. Council passes byelaw requiring syndicates and members' agents to submit annual reports in February. Council passes new audit rules in December.

1985 Membership requirements consultative document (Bird Working Party) issued in January. Underwriting Agency byelaw passed in March. Rules on binding authorities and correspondents issued in August.

1986 Business commences in new Room May 27.

THE LLOYD'S MARKET

Lloyd's of London is:–
   (a) *A Society*, incorporated under Act of Parliament of 1871, which provides the premises, a wide variety of services, administrative staff and other facilities to enable the Lloyd's Market to carry on insurance business efficiently;
   (b) *An insurance market* where with few exceptions, (notably long-term life and financial guarantee business), any insurable risk can be placed with Lloyd's underwriters through Lloyd's brokers.

ORGANISATION OF THE MARKET

Insurances are placed *at* Lloyd's with members of the Society—not *with* the Corporation of Lloyd's. These underwriting members alone are entitled to accept insurance business.

In the 18th century underwriters carried on their business singly and each man accepted risks for himself alone. In more recent years members joined together in groups called syndicates so that the resources of a large number of underwriters were combined into a single unit. This arrangement enabled them to deal in much larger sums than before and also widened their scope enormously.

Each syndicate is managed by an underwriting agent, whose

39

representative sits at his box in the Room and accepts business on behalf of the members of the syndicate. Each syndicate member is individually liable to the full extent of his private means for his own share of risks accepted; he is not liable in respect of other members' shares. Some agents underwrite for more than one syndicate.

There are four principal markets at Lloyd's; marine, non-marine, aviation and motor.

The Marine Market is the oldest at Lloyd's, and still regarded as the leading world marine market, covering anything from oil production platforms to yachts, dating back 300 years to the coffee house days.

The Non-Marine Market owes its great expansion to Cuthbert Heath who in the 1890s introduced earthquake, burglary, loss of profits and jewellers' block policies, etc. and today this market accounts for nearly half the premium income of Lloyd's underwriters.

The Aviation Market provides insurance for all types of aircraft from helicopters, jumbo jets and Concorde, to passenger liabilities and communications satellites.

The Motor Market covers all facets of the insurance of road vehicles in the UK and certain territories overseas. It is estimated that more than one in seven British private motorists are insured at Lloyd's.

LLOYD'S BROKERS

All business is brought to Lloyd's by authorised firms of Lloyd's Brokers who are not restricted to dealing with Lloyd's underwriters, but may place business with insurance companies as well. The Lloyd's Act 1982 provides that Lloyd's Brokers and Lloyd's managing agents should not have common owners and requires all such links to be dissolved by July, 1987.

The client goes to the broker and gives him details of his insurance requirements. The broker advises the client on the type of cover he wants and puts brief details of the risk on a slip. Having made out the slip the broker goes into the market and approaches one or more leading underwriters who specialise in the type of risk he is trying to place. The underwriter asks the broker questions on the risk and suggests a rate of premium. Bargaining may take place with the broker trying to get the best terms for his client. When a premium rate is agreed, the underwriter "takes a line" by writing on the slip the share of the risk he is prepared to accept for his syndicate together with the premium and his initials. Once the broker has got the risk started by a recognised "lead" he can then approach other underwriters to take a share and to sign at the same rate until he completes the cover.

The broker may "over complete" the risk in order to provide for any future increase in sums insured or limits of liability which may be required and to give as many underwriters as possible the chance to go on the risk; each syndicate's proportion is afterwards scaled down so that the total coverage is finally 100%.

The broker operates at all times in the interest of his client and must understand his requirements and advise on the best way to meet them; it is his duty to obtain the best possible terms for his clients whether at Lloyd's or in the insurance company market in London or elsewhere or both. Should there be a claim the broker arranges the settlement, collects the money from the underwriters and pays it out in the appropriate quarter.

The premium income of Lloyd's underwriters, depends on the energy and enterprise of the brokers working in harmony with the judgment and experience of the underwriters.

Lloyd's underwriters draw their business from every continent and most countries of the world; there are few places in which it is not possible to find firms or individuals with contacts among Lloyd's brokers through whom business can be placed at Lloyd's.

THE MEMBERS

Persons wishing to become members must have their application sponsored by two existing underwriting members of Lloyd's and must show that they are persons of sufficient wealth and over 21 years of age. This application can only be made through a registered Members' Agent. Candidates, who may be men or women of any nationality, go before a Rota Committee for interview and, if approved, their applications are then considered at a subsequent meeting of the full Committee. Election is by ballot.

Prior to election a member pays his entrance fee and lodges certain deposits with the Council of Lloyd's. The deposits are part of the security underlying the Lloyd's insurance policy. Deposits are held under deeds of trust which provide that the funds shall be available solely for the purpose of meeting members' underwriting liabilities. The premium income which may be underwritten on behalf of any member is determined in proportion to that member's individual deposit and by the amount of his means. The proportion also varies depending on the nationality and residence of the member.

Members of Lloyd's come from all walks of life and are also called Names. Those not involved in day-to-day business at Lloyd's are defined as external members, while those working at Lloyd's defined as working members.

Members must pay an annual subscription, based on their premium limits, and this is collected through the managing agents acting for them. These fees are used by the Council of Lloyd's to defray the Corporation of Lloyd's expenses.

All underwriting premiums received by a member of Lloyd's must be in a Premium Trust Fund either in the United States for dollar premiums or Canada for Canadian dollar premiums, or in the United Kingdom for other premiums. Only claims, R/I premiums, expenses and ascertained profits may be paid from these funds which are administered by trustees, one of whom is the member's underwriting agent.

In addition to a member's deposit and his premium trust fund, a portion of the profits earned is often retained in trust for a member as an additional reserve against underwriting losses. This reserve may take the form of a personal reserve agreed with the underwriting agent or a Special Reserve Fund created according to conditions agreed by the UK Board of Inland Revenue.

THE CORPORATION OF LLOYD'S

The Society of Lloyd's was incorporated by Act of Parliament in the year 1871. The Act provided inter alia, for the objects of the Society, the establishment of a Committee, and the making of bye-laws. Further Acts were passed in 1911, 1925 and 1951 and on 23rd July 1982 the most recent, Lloyd's Act 1982, received Royal Assent.

The Corporation of Lloyd's does not underwrite insurance business. Its function is to provide the premises, services, and assistance necessary for the conduct of underwriting, and to regulate the operation of the market place.

LLOYD'S ACT 1982

This Act has repealed many of the provisions of the earlier Acts. It has given effect to the central recommendations of the Fisher Working Party, which reported in 1980, having been appointed by the Committee of Lloyd's in 1978 to enquire into self-regulation at Lloyd's.

The Act provided for the establishment of the Council of Lloyd's, charged with overall responsibility for and control of the affairs of the Society, including, specifically, all rule-making and disciplinary powers, hitherto vested in the membership as a whole. It also required the Council to establish by byelaw a Disciplinary Committee (or Committees) and an Appeal Tribunal.

Whilst there are certain other mandatory provisions, such as the divestment of ownership of managing agencies by Lloyd's brokers (and vice versa) within a five-year period, the 1982 Act was, essentially, an enabling measure, providing a framework for the regulation of the society. Following the first meeting of the Council of Lloyd's on 5th January, 1983, all provisions of the Act are now in force.

COUNCIL OF LLOYD'S

The Council of Lloyd's comprises twenty-eight members (twenty-seven were provided for under the 1982 Act, but this number was increased by byelaw).

There are sixteen working members of the Council, elected from and by the working members of the Society. A working member is a member of the Society who occupies himself principally with the conduct of the business of insurance at Lloyd's by a Lloyd's broker or underwriting agent or who did so occupy himself immediately before retirement. Working members of the Council serve a four-year term of office, four such members retiring annually.

Eight external members of the Council are elected from and by the external members of the Society. An external member is defined as being a member of the Society who is not a working member of the Society. So far as their terms of office are concerned, each external member of the Council serves a four-year term of office, two such members retiring annually.

There are four nominated members of the Council—the number was increased by byelaw from the three provided for by the Act. These members are appointed by the Council, but any such appointment requires confirmation by the Governor of the Bank of England. Three of the nominated members serve a three-year term of office, one retiring annually. The fourth nominated member, however, is also holder of the office of Deputy Chairman and Chief Executive of the Society and special considerations apply to his terms of office.

The Act requires the annual appointment by the Council of a Chairman and two or more Deputy Chairmen of the Council, to be chosen from amongst the working members of the Council.

COMMITTEE OF LLOYD'S

The sixteen working members of the Council of Lloyd's constitute the Committee of Lloyd's. The Committee is required to elect a Chairman and two or more Deputy Chairmen.

POWERS OF THE COUNCIL

The Act states that the Council shall have the management and superintendence of the affairs of the Society and the power to regulate and direct the business of insurance at Lloyd's, and provides that it may make such byelaws as may seem requisite or expedient.

In order to pass (or amend or revoke) a byelaw a special resolution is required, that is, separate majorities both of the working members of the Council and of the external and nominated members of the Council. 500 members of the Society may require the submission of any byelaw, amendment to or revocation thereof to a General Meeting. If a resolution to revoke a byelaw or amendment thereto, or to annul a revocation thereof is passed by a majority of the members voting at such General Meeting, which majority must comprise at least one-third of the total membership of the Society, then the revocation or annulment will take effect.

All existing byelaws made under Lloyd's Acts 1871 and 1951 continue in full force and effect unless and until revoked by the Council.

DIVISION OF RESPONSIBILITIES BETWEEN COUNCIL AND COMMITTEE

The Council may by special resolution delegate to the Committee of Lloyd's (and indeed to the Chairman and Deputy Chairmen of Lloyd's and Chairman and Deputy Chairmen of the Committee) such powers or functions under Lloyd's Act 1982 as are not required to be exercised by special resolution. The precise division of responsibility can only be determined over a period of time. The Fisher Working Party envisaged, however, that the Council would perform an important role in long-term planning and in the formulation of policy, whilst the Committee would be largely concerned with day-to-day affairs.

CORPORATION DEPARTMENTS

The Council/Committee are supported in their work by permanent staff of some 2,000. Some of these also provide a direct service to members of the market. One group of departments, e.g. Advisory, Brokers, Underwriting Agents, Members' Solvency and Security, Deposits and Membership assist the Council in self-regulatory matters, whilst Publicity and Information deal with public relations and Legislation and Taxation Departments assist in relations with the United Kingdom and foreign Governments. Others, e.g. Finance, Premises, Superintendent of the Room, Captains' Room and Systems and Communications Group, provide general services to the whole of the Lloyd's community, whilst the third group, e.g. the Lloyd's Policy Signing Office, the Lloyd's Underwriters' Claims and Recoveries Office, the Aviation and Agency Departments, work closely with and largely for Underwriters in the market.

The departments within the Regulatory Services Group cover all aspects of regulation and control of the security behind the Lloyd's policy. The functions of the Advisory Department are either of a legal nature or as an information source, the Accounting and Auditing Review Department is responsible for preparing the Statutory Statement of Business/Global Accounts, for ensuring that the Syndicate Accounting Rules are complied with and for the monitoring of syndicate premium income, and the Brokers Department is concerned with Lloyd's broking companies and is responsible for new applications, changes to structures and monitoring of companies. A similar function relating to underwriting agents is the responsibility of the Underwriting Agents Department. The Members' Solvency and Security Department is concerned with the solvency requirements of members and syndicates.

The Membership Department receives, processes and monitors applications for membership. The day to day maintenance of members' deposits is undertaken by the Deposits Department.

The Publicity and Information Department advises the Council and Committee of Lloyd's and the market on all aspects of public and press relations.

The Finance Group is responsible for the wide range of financial services to the market.

The Aviation Department has a responsibility to provide survey and intelligence services to the market. Both accident investigation and pre-insurance surveys are carried out.

The Agency Department is primarily responsible for the appointment and control of the world-wide network of Lloyd's Agents.

The Solicitors Department provides legal advice and assistance to the Corporation and the market.

The Legislation Department operates for the benefit of Lloyd's underwriters by protecting their freedom to continue to transact overseas business.

The Taxation Department negotiates and/or intervenes with national taxation authorities on points of principle and practice relevant to names, and is also concerned with the tax computations of the Corporation.

The role of the Systems and Communications Group is to manage the day-to-day data processing activities of the Corporation, to advise Corporation management and the Lloyd's market on the systems necessary to enable Lloyd's to cope with future activities and to develop any systems the Council decides are necessary.

The Superintendent of the Room's department ensures the smooth running of the Underwriting Room.

SELF REGULATION AT LLOYD'S

The effectiveness of any form of regulation depends upon the general willingness of society to obey the law and respect the sanctions which the regulatory body is prepared to enforce. There are broadly two ways to do this: statutory regulation and self-regulation.

Self-regulation differs in essence from statutory regulation in that it is a system of rule-making devised and operated by those to whom the rules are to be applied. Such regulation is thus of limited scope, designed to apply to members of a clearly defined group and to regulate the activities of the members of that group. As well

46

as prescribing specific rules, it is concerned to lay down standards of conduct which a statute could not easily embrace.

The objectives identified by the Working Party chaired by Sir Henry Fisher which reported in 1980 in relation to the proper regulation of Lloyd's were, "the maintenance of the security of the Lloyd's policy, the maintenance of the highest standards of conduct and integrity by all users of the Market, the preservation of Lloyd's as a Market where conditions of free competition can obtain, and the maintenance of standards of fair treatment for those members of the Lloyd's community who can reasonably look to the Committee for protection."

There is a feature of Lloyd's not mentioned in the passage from the Fisher report which nevertheless strongly influences both the form and substance of regulation at Lloyd's and that is the pervasive existence of agency relationships within the Market. Names can only underwrite insurance business through the under-writing agents, whom they appoint to look after their affairs, and insurance business may only be brought to Lloyd's via Lloyd's brokers who are the agent of the insured. Lloyd's regulations must both take account of and reinforce the standards required of an agent without appearing to replace them.

Lloyd's operates through a Committee structure both for the development of rules and their implementation. In this way it ensures that the necessary blend of skills, knowledge and opinion are brought into play. These Committees, are normally chaired by a member of Council and their work is reported to the Council of Lloyd's on a regular basis.

The Committees are in the main responsible for policy develop-ment; for example the Accounting and Auditing Standards Committee and the Solvency and Security Committee in relation to the matters which their titles evidently refer. Others however, have executive responsibilities; the Investigations Committee and the Underwriting Agents Registration Committee are good ex-amples. The membership of each Committee is chosen to reflect the task that it has to perform and may include in addition to members of Council:
— Senior members of the Corporation staff
— Senior Market figures
— Representatives from outside the Lloyd's Market e.g. from accounting or legal firms.

The work of the Committees is supported by the Corporation staff who are also responsible for the day to day monitoring of the rules.

Various types of 'rules' have been developed under the specific and general powers contained in the Lloyd's Act: these are:–

Primary rules, that is, byelaws and regulations;

Secondary rules which encompass Explanatory Notes and Codes of Practice.

Primary Rules

Primary rules are designed
— to create disciplinary offences;
— to cover matters of principle which are fundamental to Lloyd's;
— to lay down administrative powers and procedures, for example, composition and proceeding of the Council;
— to clarify the powers of the Council, the Committee and others
  involved in regulation.

A primary rule may be either a byelaw or a regulation:–
— a *byelaw* is passed by special resolution of the Council and
  requires majority support from the Working, the External and
  the Nominated Members;
— a *regulation* is passed by the Committee of Lloyd's on specific
  delegated powers from the Council, and is concerned with the
  'business of insurance at Lloyd's'.
Byelaws and regulations may be made independently from each other or may be interrelated. For example, a byelaw may be passed which is widely drawn and expressed in general terms. Thereafter a regulation is drawn up to assist in the detailed application and interpretation of the byelaw in specific Market circumstances.

Secondary Rules

The policy of the Council is to avoid, in so far as possible, detailed primary rules and to keep the content of byelaws and regulations to a minimum. Many of Lloyd's byelaws are enabling in nature and are confirmed to the general principles involved. Secondary rules are designed to back up, or fill in the detail of, such primary rules and to be capable of speedy amendment. This structure permits the general principle expressed in the primary rules to survive without alteration for some time and for secondary rules to be expanded or amended as and when policy changes occur or problems arise.

There are two classes of secondary rules currently in usage:–

First, there are explanatory notes. Although not 'rules' as such, explanatory notes form part of the regulatory structure and are issued to explain the intention of a primary rule, to indicate the criteria that will be used to judge particular matters, e.g. the suitability of Underwriting Members or of directors of underwriting agents and, where discretionary powers are provided for in the primary rule, to indicate when consent to a proposal is likely to be given.

Second, there are codes of practice. Again, these are not strictly 'rules' in that they do not categorically prohibit or require. The purpose of a code of practice is to try to raise the standards of those covered by the code to those of the best and spell out those standards of behaviour which it would be in the interests of the Lloyd's community to achieve. No disciplinary action would flow from breach of the provisions of a code although regard would be had to its contents in any disciplinary proceedings.

New Subordinate Legislation

Forty byelaws, thirteen amendments thereto, four regulations and two codes of practice were made under the Lloyd's Act, 1982 during the period 5th January, 1982 to the end of October 1986.

The new rules have covered many topics but the subordinate legislation can generally be categorised under five headings:–
(i)   investigatory and discipline
(ii)   membership
(iii) divestment and registration of underwriting agents
(iv)   accounting and disclosure; and
(vi)   rules to deal with conflicts of interest
In due course formal rules for Lloyd's brokers will be formulated.

General Review Department

The General Review Department was established within the Corporation in October 1986, to monitor compliance with Lloyd's regulations by underwriting agents and Lloyd's brokers.

The department is responsible for periodic reviews of underwriting agents and Lloyd's brokers to confirm that adequate systems and procedures are operating to ensure compliance with Lloyd's byelaws and regulations. Its staff liaise closely with other departments within the Corporation's Regulatory Services Group and its terms of reference enable the department to recommend changes or improvements to the existing regulatory structure.

Under the provisions of the Review Powers Byelaw, the Deputy Chairman and Chief Executive of Lloyd's are empowered to order a review of the affairs, or any aspect of the affairs of a Lloyd's broker or underwriting agent, not necessarily limited to monitoring compliance with Lloyd's rules.

The byelaw, gives powers when a review has been ordered to require directors and staff of agencies and brokers to provide information, produce documents, and allow access to their premises by members of the Review Department. Normally, reasonable notice is required to be given before these powers are exercised. But the byelaw also enables the Deputy Chairman and the Chief Executive to direct that powers be exercised without prior notice, when it appears expedient for him to do so.

ii) THE MEMBERS OF LLOYD'S; THEIR UNLIMITED LIABILITY

SECURITY UNDERLYING POLICIES AT LLOYD'S

Requirements of Membership

These requirements are applicable to New Names elected to commence underwriting with effect from January 1st, 1988 and to existing Names who change their underwriting arrangements after January 1st, 1987.

Category	Means (£10,000 increases)	Gross Premium Underwriting Limit Maximum (£25,000 increases)	Deposit as % of GPUL	Minimum Deposit
		£30,000		£12,000
Lloyd's Names	Nominal	£50,000	40%	£20,000
		£75,000		£30,000
Lloyd's & Connected & Associated Names* Resident & Domiciled in U.K.	£30,000 (Minimum) To £70,000 (Maximum)	£175,000	30%	£22,500
Connected & Associated Names* Resident or Domiciled Outside U.K.	£30,000 (Minimum) To £70,000 (Maximum)	£175,000	40%	£30,000
Members Resident and Domiciled in U.K.	£100,000 (Minimum) To £520,000 (Maximum)	£1,300,000	20%	£20,000
Members resident or Domiciled Outside U.K.	£100,000 (Minimum) To £520,000 (Maximum)	£1,300,000	28%	£28,000

*Includes Names on reduced Means.
+ Gross Premium Underwriting Limit not to exceed 2.5 times Means shown.

All existing members, whether changing their underwriting arrangements or not and all new Names commencing underwriting from 1 January, 1988, will be required to bring their means and deposits into line with current requirements by 1 January, 1988. From this date, the "franchise" which is 30% for reinsurance purposes will also be absorbed into the Gross Premium Underwriting Limit. The "franchise" is an addition to the overall premium limit allowed for underwriting purposes.

The means test is a continuing requirement during the time a member remains active in underwriting at Lloyd's and members are required to confirm their means periodically and to notify the Committee of Lloyd's should their net worth fall below the required level as a result of their own act or omission. If a member is unable to satisfy the Committee at any time regarding their means, the Committee may require the member to cease underwriting or reduce their premium income limit for such period as they think fit. Those who are actively employed full time in the Lloyd's market can be admitted as members with higher percentage deposits without having to show means but the amount of their permitted premium income is restricted. A statement of means, which must be signed by the applicant as well as by an approved bank having a branch in the United Kingdom or by a practising firm of United Kingdom solicitors, chartered or certified accountants or their associated firms, must show a minimum net worth of £100,000. This amount must be in "readily realisable" assets as defined by the Council of Lloyd's.

SECURITY BEHIND A LLOYD'S POLICY

The security behind a Lloyd's policy is unparalled for the following reason:–

Premium Trust Fund

Under the provisions of the United Kingdom Insurance Companies Acts, 1958 to 1982, underwriters are required to pay the whole of the premiums received by them in respect of their underwriting business into a trust fund out of which claims and expenses are met.

Because of Lloyd's three-year accounting system it is only after a period of not less than three years from the inception of an underwriting account that the ascertained profits are distributed from the trust funds.

Underwriting Deposits

Every underwriting member before election is required to lodge with the Council of Lloyd's a deposit consisting of cash, approved investments or a bank guarantee/letter of credit as security for the fulfilment of underwriting commitments. The amount of the deposit is fixed by the Council of Lloyd's. Member's Lloyd's deposits are not released until their underwriting liabilities have been fully reinsured by other Lloyd's underwriters.

Deposits are held under deeds of trust which provide that the funds shall be available solely for the purpose of meeting the member's underwriting liabilities.

The assets of which the deposit is comprised must be either registered in the name of the Corporation of Lloyd's or held in the name of the Corporation as trustee for the Member.

At the beginning of each calendar year any member with the agreement of their underwriting agent may increase the amount of their deposit and therefore their premium limit, provided that they are able to meet the means test required for the higher limit. A member may also be required by the Council to provide an additional security where their premium income in the previous year exceeds their total permitted premium limit.

In the event that there are insufficient monies in their premiums trust fund, the funds which the member has established in respect of their underwriting, may be used in certain circumstances towards meeting their liabilities. For this purpose, the Lloyd's deposit is divided into three parts:

1. The part of the deposit which may not be used to cover either a loss on a closed year of account or an estimated deficiency on a year of account at the end of its first or second year. This part of the deposit "failsafe" must be retained against liabilities which might arise in respect of the subsequent years of account.

2. The "first reserve" which may be used, with the approval of the Committee of Lloyd's, to cover or to meet an underwriting loss on a closed account or to cover an estimated deficiency on an account at the end of its first or second year: in the event that the first reserve is used to cover a closed year loss, the deposit must be reinstated if the member is to continue underwriting at the same level.

3. The "second reserve", being the remainder of the Lloyd's deposit, which may be used to cover an estimated deficiency on an account at the end of its first or second year only. If, for any reason, the member has to use the second reserve to cover a closed year loss they will be required to cease underwriting.

Premium Income Limits

The volume of business members may accept in any year is calculated at specified ratios of their Lloyd's deposits and qualifying means. If the premium income of members should exceed their premium limits, they must provide further deposits in proportion to the amount of overwriting and may be required to show increased means.

Premium income forms the link between the asset base of the Society and the risks assumed by its members. A system of premium limits at individual member and at syndicate level operates to maintain the necessary security ratios. It is therefore important to ensure that the premium income accepted by individual syndicates adheres to these limits stringently in order to protect both Names and policyholders.

Lloyd's requirements relating to premium income monitoring are dealt with by the Accounting and Auditing Review department and this involves ensuring that cases of actual and potential over-writing by Lloyd's syndicates are identified at the earliest stage possible and that appropriate action is instigated by the agencies concerned or where necessary by Lloyd's.

Underwriting Reserves

Most underwriting agents require their members to establish underwriting reserves in addition to their Lloyd's deposits. These funds may be in the form of personal reserves held in trust by the agent and in the case of the Special Reserve Fund in the joint trusteeship with the Corporation of Lloyd's and is approved by the Inland Revenue.

Unlimited Liability

All underwriting members are liable in respect of the risks undertaken by them to the full extent of their private wealth.

Lloyd's Central Fund

Individual members are liable for their own underwriting commit-ments and should the assets held on their behalf at Lloyd's and their personal resources prove insufficient to meet their liabilities, the resources held centrally by Lloyd's are available to meet their obligations. These latter resources comprise the Central Fund (established in 1926) to which all members pay an annual levy.

The Central Fund Byelaw provides for its use for any purpose which, in the Council's opinion, is in the interests of the members of Lloyd's as a whole in connection with their underwriting business.

The Solvency Test

The United Kingdom Insurance Companies Acts, 1958 to 1982, require all Lloyd's underwriters to submit each year to a solvency test which must be conducted by a qualified accountant approved by the Council of Lloyd's. The annual solvency test is a very searching test of solvency requiring underwriters to show that their underwriting assets at Lloyd's are sufficient to meet their underwriting liabilities.

Should any underwriters fail to reach the standard of solvency required, they must provide additional funds to the extent necessary or cease underwriting. The regulations prescribing the basis upon which the solvency test is to be conducted are reviewed annually by the Council and have to meet with the approval of the British Department of Trade and Industry.

An annual audit of underwriters' accounts was introduced by the Committee of Lloyd's as a voluntary safeguard as far back as 1908 and throughout the years and under ever-changing conditions it has proved to be the foundation upon which the security afforded by a Lloyd's policy rests. The stringent basis upon which the Lloyd's solvency test is carried out each year is accepted for legislative and other purposes as constituting adequate evidence of the solvency of Lloyd's underwriters.

Statutory Statement of Business/Global Accounts

Lloyd's is required to file annually with the Secretary of State a statement of business prepared pursuant to the Insurance Companies Act 1982. This statement is in a prescribed form and covers the underwriting results and the solvency position of the Lloyd's market as a whole. The filing of the statement is fundamental to the supervision of Lloyd's by the Department of Trade and Industry.

iii) THE GROUPING OF THESE MEMBERS IN SYNDICATES AND THE BASIC ROLE OF UNDERWRITING AGENTS

THE GROUPING OF MEMBERS IN SYNDICATES

The syndicate system developed from a practice which was common enough in former times whereby an underwriter would "write a line" on a policy on behalf of one or two acquaintances who might have lacked the time or skill to sit in person at Lloyd's. With the development of marine insurance as a profession came an increase in the number of those employing an underwriter to act for them. In the 1840s, the Committee insisted that all whose names appeared on a Lloyd's policy, whether underwriting in person or through an agent, should be elected members of the Society. This was one of the first of many steps taken to strengthen Lloyd's policies whose security today is unparallelled.

Early syndicates were small and reflected the relatively modest amount of business available to the market in those days. The big underwriting syndicates of today are a direct result of Lloyd's great expansion in the last ninety years. In spite of dire predictions to the contrary, the new non-marine risks of the 1880s proved very profitable and one or two enterprising men at Lloyd's found themselves underwriting for larger syndicates than had ever been seen before. The non-marine market rapidly expanded and, with premiums flowing from all parts of the world, Lloyd's underwriters were able to cover the increasing volume of business only by accepting an ever-growing number of names into their syndicates.

Each member may join one or more syndicates. At present there are over 400 such syndicates. Each syndicate has its own professional underwriter and a staff who have the responsibility of accepting risks, fixing premium rates and authorizing the payment of claims on behalf of the members in the syndicate. Each member gives such underwriters authority to underwrite insurance risks for him and the underwriter may delegate this authority in certain circumstances. Such underwriters receive salaries and often, a profit commission for their services. A syndicate is composed of members who have similarly authorized a particular underwriter. Within each syndicate each individual member takes a percentage commitment of the risks underwritten by the members of the syndicate. The liability of each member in the syndicate is several and not joint. In other words, every member is bound to each risk underwritten "each for his own part and not one for another".

Whilst in the early days of Lloyd's each Underwriter underwrote his own risks, the development of syndicates resulted in the current practice of each member appointing an Underwriting Agent or Agents, who employ an underwriter to write business for all the members of the syndicate or, alternatively, delegate the underwriting to another underwriting agent under a Sub-Agency Agreement.

DUTIES AND FUNCTIONS OF UNDERWRITING AGENTS

A Lloyd's underwriting agent, which must be a partnership or limited company and not a sole trader acts as the link between the underwriting syndicates, and the Names. All Lloyd's underwriting agents are scrutinized by Lloyd's before being added to the register of approved agents. Underwriting Agents fall into two categories—Members' Agents and Managing Agents and the Register contains appropriate details of the scope of the approval given. Applications for approval give full details of how the agency will be set up, the management, the shareholding together with detailed information as to the experience and history of all concerned, the number of Names who will be underwriting through the agent and details of syndicates to be managed in the case of Managing Agents. An Underwriting agency must be two thirds controlled by members of Lloyd's who underwrite through the Agency and at least two thirds of the partners or directors must be members of Lloyd's, who underwrite through the Agency and are principally occupied in the Underwriting Agency business or as Lloyd's Brokers in the case of Members' Agents.

Members' Agents

A members' agent undertakes the recruitment of new Names, the administration and servicing of existing names, the compliance with the various regulations and requirements which affect their Names, placing the member on a syndicate (subject to the member's agreement) and acting as liaison between the Corporation and the member. An applicant is free to approach other agents if he so wishes, but the actual application for membership of Lloyd's must be handled by one agent. It is permissible to have a separate agent for each class of business—marine, non-marine, motor and aviation and so on. In these cases one of the agents must be appointed the co-ordinating agent. This holds no special privileges other than that the co-ordinating agent is responsible for handling the candidate's application for membership, and for agreeing the Name's overall premium limit position with the Council and Committee of Lloyd's.

An application for membership may only be made through a registered members' agent, who will provide the candidate with the necessary forms and will guide the candidate through the application procedures. Applications may be made at any time during the year, but only those received prior to 30 June will allow a member to start underwriting on the following 1 January. All documentation in relation to membership for an underwriting year must be completed by the preceding 30 November. As part of this procedure, the candidate must attend a Rota Committee interview at Lloyd's, when a representative of the Council of Lloyd's will ensure that the candidate is fully aware of the requirements and risks involved in membership.

A candidate must be sponsored by two existing members of Lloyd's, one of whom must be a director/partner or employee of the proposed members' agent. The candidate's principal sponsor is required to demonstrate a sufficient knowledge of the candidate. A number of members' agents make it a practice to remunerate sponsors or other intermedaries. Such remuneration may be continuing and is required to be disclosed to the candidate.

There is a non-refundable entrance fee payable to Lloyd's by 30 November in the year of application and thereafter an annual subscription, based on a member's premium income limit, is charged by Lloyd's.

The agent is responsible for briefing the candidate on the full background and responsibilities of membership of Lloyd's, and he must assist the candidates in preparing their applications. Among the information which has to be provided to the candidate is:

—a full description of the agency and of Lloyd's;
—past result figures:
—details of the business written by the syndicates that the candidate is proposing to join.

During the last stages of the application, the candidate has to confirm to Lloyd's that all the necessary information has been forthcoming from the agent, so that the Committee of Lloyd's can be satisfied that the agent has dealt with the application in the correct manner and made all the required disclosures to the applicant.

It is also a function of the members' agent to review the underwriting arrangements of each existing Name every year in the light of the policies and results of the various syndicates, to ensure a proper spread of risk and to consider any particular Name's requirements.

Each Name signs a standard underwriting agency agreement with his agent which gives that agent the power to underwrite for the Name, and to comply both with any Lloyd's regulations and any statutory requirements. It also establishes the duties of the agent, and the obligations of the Name, including the remuneration which he will pay to the agent.

A members' agent is empowered to appoint the trustees of the Lloyd's Premiums Trust Fund, but, in practice, normally delegates this power to the managing agent.

The members' agent is responsibile for maintaining the Names' special and personal reserve funds and the investments are normally purchased at the request of the Name.

Managing Agents

Each syndicate at Lloyd's is run by a managing agent. Some managing agents may be responsible for several syndicates of similar or different classes, each of which will have its own separate identity for administrative and accounting purposes.

As a syndicate Manager, it produces the annual accounts of the syndicates, reflecting profits or losses made.

Each managing agency has an agreement with one or more members' agencies that they will provide some members on each of their syndicates.

The underwriter manages the underwriting box and the agent manages the administration of the syndicate and is responsible to and for all the Names who participate in the syndicate.

It is a contractual obligation for the managing agents to supply regular underwriting figures to the members' agent concerned to give an indication of the progress of the particular year of account. These figures are the total cumulative amounts for premiums and claims for the open years of account under the terms of the agreements.

At the close of each year of account syndicate accounts are drawn up by the managing agent not only for the closing year but also for the open years (normally two). The reinsurance to close the account will be calculated in accordance with the regulations set down by Lloyd's and will be agreed with the syndicate auditors who carry out the Lloyd's solvency test in accordance with annually reviewed regulations agreed between the Department of Trade and Industry and Lloyd's. Every Name must pass this solvency test in order to continue underwriting.

In addition to conducting the solvency test, the auditor provides annual premium income figures for each syndicate as required by Lloyd's. The managing agent is responsible for ensuring that the amount of business written for a syndicate is within the premium income limits allocated by its members to that syndicate. If a Name's total premium income for all his syndicates should exceed his premium income limit in any year he can be required by

Lloyd's to provide additional security or to reduce his underwriting commitment.

Each Name on the syndicate receives a copy of the audited accounts together with a statement of his personal account for the closed year, showing his profit or loss for that year. Managing agents are responsible for the distribution of the accounts, to their own direct Names on their syndicate and to the members' agents concerned.

The Syndicate Accounting Rules set out the manner in which managing agents are to report to Names.

iv) THE POSITION OF LLOYD'S BROKERS IN RELATION TO THE SOCIETY—REQUIREMENTS TO BE A "LLOYD'S BROKING" FIRM

LLOYD'S BROKERS

Contracts of insurance at Lloyd's cannot be effected directly between the proposer and the Lloyd's underwriters (except for direct motor dealing). They can only be transacted through intermediaries styled Lloyd's Brokers who are subject to the overall control of the Insurance Brokers (Registration) Act 1977. Sections 3(3) and 4(4) of the Act grant Lloyd's brokers special rights concerning registration and enrolment while day to day control is exercised both by the Council and Committee of Lloyd's and by the Lloyd's Insurance Brokers' Committee of the British Insurance Brokers' Association.

Part V of SI 1979 No 489 exempts Lloyd's Brokers from Section 11 (Accounts etc.) of the Registration Act.

Part IV of SI 1979 No 408 exempts Lloyd's Brokers from Part II (Professional Indemnity Insurance) according to Section 12 of the Registration Act. There is no exemption for Lloyd's brokers from Part III (Grants Scheme), in respect of which the enabling legislation is section 12(g) of the Registration Act.

The principals of any firm desiring to be admitted as Lloyd's brokers must satisfy the Council and Committee of Lloyd's as to the solvency of their firm as well as their competence and familiarity with the Lloyd's market.

The company must be incorporated in the E.E.C. and able, through offices in London, to service the Lloyd's Market and its policyholders.

The company must employ in London an adequate number of directors and staff with experience in the Lloyd's Market, (i.e. Broking in the Room, Claims procedures, Terms of Credit, Central Accounting settlements, policy preparation, etc.).

A deposit (£10,000) is payable by all Lloyd's brokers on admission and held in trust under a security deed by Lloyd's. It is intended to contribute towards any unpaid debts to Lloyd's underwriters.

Permissible assets must exceed liabilities by a solvency margin of 10 per cent of net retained brokerage (subject to a minimum of £25,000).

Net retained brokerage is brokerage retained by a broker after allowances to third parties have been deducted. However, for margin of solvency purposes, NRB includes all fees, incomes and charges receivable in respect of services rendered or expenditure incurred.

Where the paid-up share capital (represented by tangible net assets) of a Lloyd's broker on admission is less than £100,000 the shareholding directors of the ultimate holding company must furnish an unlimited guarantee in respect of the liabilities of the Lloyd's broker to its insurance creditors.

A Lloyd's broking company must not be reliant upon on predominant source of business even when that source of business is a state or national insurance corporation.

"One predominant source" will normally be interpreted as being more than 20% of the applicant broker's net retained brokerage which emanates from a single source or from a "tied" or "or in house" arrangement. It will not be regarded as a breach of this rule where the single source is a broking company in the same group as the applicant, provided that the business channelled through that single source arises from a larger number of original sources.

The one outlet rule states that a Lloyd's broker must be able to demonstrate, and be able to continue to demonstrate, that it can reasonably expect not to be unduly reliant in any one financial year upon any one body corporate carrying on insurance business or any one Lloyd's syndicate in the placing of its business.

Shareholdings by both insurance interests and non-insurance interests in Lloyd's brokers are controlled. For shareholdings by insurance interests the general rule is that shareholdings in a Lloyd's broker by non-Lloyd's insurance interests (whether directly or through other companies or persons in the groups) be limited to 20% of the total share capital and in the case of unquoted companies such shareholding should be in non-voting shares. Any new holders of 20% or more of the total share capital (where specifically agreed) should give a Letter or Undertaking in the prescribed form regarding the independence of the Lloyd's broker. As regards non-insurance interests all new holders of 20% or more of the capital are required to give a Letter of Undertaking.

A company applying to be admitted as a Lloyd's broking firm need not necessarily handle all classes of insurance and reinsurance but it must make acceptable arrangements with another Lloyd's Broker for dealing with enquiries and the handling of insurance if the applicants themselves do not handle such business.

With the exception of the acceptance of risks and issuance of documents under binding authorities and some services in claims negotiations and issuing certificates in motor insurance the broker is always the agent of the insured in Lloyd's transactions. All the common law duties of disclosure and utmost good faith apply to brokers as well as insurers in contracts of non-marine insurance at Lloyd's, while for marine contracts these duties are made statutory by the Marine Insurance Act 1906.

v) THE ROLE AND RESPONSIBILITY OF AN APPOINTED UNDERWRITER OF A SYNDICATE

Underwriting at Lloyd's coffee house began as a purely personal business. Individual persons, who became known as Underwriters, accepted risks entirely for their own personal account, backing their own judgment by risking their own fortunes, and provided the premiums they charged exceeded the claims they were called upon to pay, they retained the profit for themselves.

When such an Underwriter was successful, it was attractive both to him and to his friends that he should accept risk not only for himself but also for one or two of them as well, risking their fortunes exactly as he was risking his own, and taking an agreed commission on any profit he made for them.

In this setting the Underwriter's duty is obvious and simple, and his fulfilment of that duty is virtually automatic. He is doing his very best for himself; his friends interests are identical with his own, so he is doing his very best for them as well. His duty to behave honourably to his clients, the insured, is also self interest, for without a reputation for fair dealing nobody would wish to trade with him.

The growth of the syndicate system at Lloyd's, the development of the agency system through to the separation of the Names' agents and the managing agent's function leading to the active Underwriter being employed by the managing agent—albeit as a director or partner—have all caused the active Underwriter to be increasingly distanced from the individuals, his Names, on whose behalf he accepts risks.

Ask any responsible Underwriter at Lloyd's where his paramount duty lies, the unhesitating reply will always be "to my Names". It is the Names' fortunes which are at risk, and whilst no-one can eliminate risk from insurance—which is a risk business—the Underwriter must do all in his power to keep the risk of loss down to an acceptable level, both as to likelihood and quantum.

The Underwriter has a duty to the principals in addition to common law duties as an agent and will have fiduciary duties and trustee duties.

The Underwriter's duty to the Society of Lloyd's as a whole is at once simple and complex. Simple because honourable behaviour, in its fullest sense, covers all that is required. Complex because there are so many parties to whom a duty is owed. Lloyd's prospers on its financial security and commercial integrity. In spite of the fact that within the Society individual syndicates are in competition with each other, the broker/underwriter relationship is partially adversarial and partly symbiotic, broker competes with broker, and the Council is sovereign to a subject but democratic society, nonetheless, all members owe a duty to the whole. The Underwriter is therefore not in the position of competing to the death with fellow Lloyd's underwriters, but of competing on a basis which does not undermine the market's structure or reputation.

In carrying out his duties, the Underwriter controls the insurance business of his syndicate. This can be broken down into various sections:–

(1) *Underwriting Policy.* The underwriter must determine the areas of business in which he wishes to be involved, and establish guidelines as to insurance conditions and premium rates. He must establish the size of lines he wishes to write, bearing in mind the syndicates's premium income and the nature and quality of the individual risk. He is responsible for

ensuring that the amount of business accepted does not exceed his syndicate's premium limit.

(2) *Market Disciplines.* The Underwriter is responsible for his syndicate's compliance with Lloyd's regulations, market agreements, codes of conduct and market practice, both in relation to the business he accepts and in other areas of the conduct of business.

(3) *Records.* Syndicates must keep full and accurate records of the business they accept, and the Underwriter must arrange for statistics to be created from those records to provide the necessary information for effective control of the account.

(4) *Reinsurance.* All syndicates need to be protected from catastrophic losses, and the Underwriter must arrange and manage a reinsurance programme to give prudent protection at affordable cost.

(5) *Claims.* Although much of the responsibility for handling claims is delegated to the market claims offices, the ultimate responsibility for claims matters rests with the Underwriter, and he must always be satisfied that they are being dealt with to his satisfaction.

(6) *Market bodies.* The operation of the Lloyd's market relies very heavily on the co-operation of Underwriters in various committes, working parties, etc., and Underwriters are expected to play their part in supporting these bodies.

(7) *Reinsurance to Close.* The profit or loss of an underwriting year of account may not be struck until the account has run for 36 months. To do this a premium must be established to provide for claims, known and unknown, which still have to be paid. The evaluation of this risk is of paramount importance to the syndicate assuming the liability.

vi) MARKET ASSOCIATIONS

MARKET ASSOCIATIONS

Lloyd's Underwriters' Association

Lloyd's Underwriters' Association which was formed in 1909, acts officially for marine underwriters at Lloyd's in all technical matters relating to their business. It neither effects nor underwrites marine insurances. The Association's membership comprises all Lloyd's marine underwriters.

The Committee of the Association meets regularly to discuss the underwriting and general administrative problems which affect the great variety of insurance that is written in the marine market. It frequently makes recommendations to all members of the Association with a view to improving the efficiency and profitability of their market. Also, the Association keeps its members supplied with all pertinent information that is likely to have some bearing upon the underwriting of marine insurance at Lloyd's.

The Association acts in close liaison with Lloyd's Insurance Brokers' Committee, the Institute of London Underwriters and Liverpool Underwriters' Association, and appoints Lloyd's representatives to serve on various joint committees which deliberate upon problems that are common both to the Lloyd's and Company marine markets. It is also represented on the International Union of Marine Insurance.

Lloyd's Underwriters' Non-Marine Association

In 1910 Lloyd's Underwriters' Non-Marine Association was formed "with the object of meeting periodically to consider matters relating to fire and Non-Marine business at Lloyd's." One of the chief functions of that Association was then, and still is, to circulate information to non-marine underwriters relating to non-marine business throughout the world. It is not however the purpose of the Association to involve itself in underwriting.

On a broader front the Association collaborates with the Committee of Lloyd's in seeking to keep doors open for Lloyd's underwriters to do non-marine business in all countries throughout the world and to open doors which have for one reason or another been shut. The Non-marine market can bring to bear on an insurance problem which emerges in one particular country the experience and expertise which the market has probably already gained in that field in other parts of the world.

Membership of the Association comprises all the active non-marine underwriters at Lloyd's underwriting for Non-Marine Syndicates. They elect a Committee of 12 and are joined by the non-marine members of the Committee of Lloyd's and the Chairman and Deputy Chairmen of Lloyd's ex-officio. There are very many sub-committees which consider in great detail all the problems of the non-marine marketplace and have incidentally produced over

1,000 "standard" policy forms and clauses for the convenience of the non-marine market. Again, it is important to emphasise that these forms are in no way mandatory and probably more business is done on underwriters' or brokers' private or tailor-made forms than on "NMA" standard forms.

Lloyd's Aviation Underwriters' Association

Lloyd's Aviation Underwriters' Association was first formed in 1935 to represent the interests of the Lloyd's aviation market. At first confined to underwriters of specialist aviation syndicates, membership was later extended to the underwriters of any Lloyd's Syndicate writing aviation business. This is reflected in the Association's Committee, which is elected by ballot annually and now consists of ten specialist and two non-specialist members, with the Chairman and Deputy Chairmen of Lloyd's and any other specialist aviation underwriters who are members of the Committee of Lloyd's as ex officio members.

The Committee acts on behalf of the members as a whole keeping them informed and sometimes making recommendations designed to improve the efficiency of the market, but does not involve itself in individual underwriting or rating problems.

The Association publishes a book of Policies and Clauses commonly used in aviation business, including the standard forms. The book is periodically brought up to date as new or revised forms are introduced. Amendments to approved wordings are normally drafted by the Joint Technical & Clauses Committee, composed of members of the LAUA and the Aviation Insurance Offices' Association.

Lloyd's Motor Underwriters' Association

With the introduction of compulsory third party insurance in 1930 the need for an Association to deal exclusively with motor business became essential, and Lloyd's Motor Underwriters' Association embarked on its independent career in June 1931. The motor car being a very mobile risk, it was not sufficient to deal solely with U.K. legislation, but to make provision for meeting the requirements of compulsory insurance laws in overseas territories, particularly Europe. In collaboration with other UK motor insurers, the Green Card System was introduced by insurers, which provides the facility to enable a motorist to satisfy the compulsory insurance requirements of foreign legislation when motoring abroad. Likewise, the Association was involved in the negotiations with the UK Government to deal with the compensation of victims of uninsured or untraced motorists, resulting in the formation of the Motor Insurers' Bureau, a pattern which has been adopted in many foreign countries. Because third party bodily injury insurance is compulsory, it is vital that motor underwriters should be fully informed on all legislation likely to affect the use of a motor car on the road.

Additionally, they must be informed on the construction and repairability of the modern car. To conduct fundamental research in this field, Lloyd's Motor Syndicates, together with the Company Market, have set up the Motor Insurance Repair Research Centre at Thatcham.

Unlike other Lloyd's Syndicates, each Motor Syndicate has an individual title whereby it can be easily and quickly identified; this makes for ease of document recognition and is of considerable convenience to the insured and the authorities.

The membership of LMUA comprises all the specialist Motor Syndicates transacting motor business in the UK and overseas and from this membership a committee is elected.

Lloyd's Underwriting Agents' Association

Membership comprises many underwriting agents. The aim is to protect the interest of agents, it has an important part to play in representing members' interests to the Council and Committee of Lloyd's and watching developments which may affect members.

British Insurance Brokers' Association
Lloyd's Insurance Brokers' Committee

The British Insurance Brokers' Association (BIBA) was established in January, 1977, having previously been known as the British Insurance Brokers' Council. The decision to form the new oganisation was taken earlier by the four former insurance broking associations (the Association of Insurance Brokers, the Corporation of Insurance Brokers, the Federation of Insurance Brokers, and Lloyd's Insurance Brokers' Association). On 1st January, 1978, the membership of the four associations was transferred to BIBA and the old organisations dissolved to leave a single national body representing the interests of insurance brokers in the United Kingdom. The purpose was to ensure that for the future united action was taken on measures to protect and promote the interests of the British insurance broking industry and that a single representative body existed able to react to or express opinion on matters affecting the industry. A principal aim of BIBA is to raise the standards of insurance broking in the United Kingdom with the intention of ensuring that new enhanced means of protecting consumer interests are made effective.

The Lloyd's Insurance Brokers' Committee is an autonomous committee of the Association. It is the direct successor of Lloyd's Insurance Brokers' Association, which was formed in 1910.

Through LIBC matters of mutual concern can be discussed with the Committee of Lloyd's, Lloyd's Underwriters and anyone else with whom Lloyd's Brokers have need to deal.

The affairs of the Committee are controlled by a Committee of 16 elected from Lloyd's Brokers' in membership of BIBA. There are four Executive Committees (Aviation, Marine, Motor and Non-Marine) the former also acting as the BIBA Aviation and Marine Committee and in further support there is a structure of 40 Sub-Committees drawn from experts in Brokers' Offices who are best equipped to reach recommendations based upon a practical knowledge of their business.

The channels of communication with Lloyd's Brokers are the speciality circular letters on a wide range of subjects which affect Lloyd's Brokers' business as well as the BIBA Bulletin and Journal ("The British Insurance Broker") and normal day to day contact in correspondence, by telephone and in meetings.

All firms of Lloyd's Brokers are Members of the Lloyd's Region of BIBA and the expenses in conducting the work on behalf of Brokers' are met in the main from subscriptions they pay.

REVISION NOTES

LLOYD'S BROKERS

All business is brought to Lloyd's by authorised firms of Lloyd's Brokers who are not restricted to dealing with Lloyd's under-writers, but may place business with insurance companies as well. The Lloyd's Act 1982 provides that Lloyd's Brokers and Lloyd's managing agents should not have common owners and requires all such links to be dissolved by July, 1987.

The Members

Persons wishing to become members must have their applications sponsored by two existing underwriting members of Lloyd's and must show that they are persons of some wealth and over 21 years of age. Candidates, who may be men or women of any nationality, go before a Rota Committee for interview and, if approved, their applications are then considered at a subsequent meeting of the Committee. Election is by ballot.

Lloyd's Act 1982

This Act has repealed many of the provisions of the earlier Acts. It has given effect to the central recommendations of the Fisher Working Party, which reported in 1980, having been appointed by the Committee of Lloyd's in 1978 to enquire into self-regulation at Lloyd's.

The Act provided for the establishment of a new Council of Lloyd's, charged with overall responsibility for and control of the affairs of the Society, including, specifically, all rule-making and disciplinary powers, hitherto vested in the membership as a whole. It also required the Council to establish by byelaw a Disciplinary Committee (or Committees) and an Appeal Tribunal.

Council of Lloyd's

The Council of Lloyd's comprises twenty-eight members (twenty-seven were provided for under the 1982 Act, but this number was increased by byelaw). (Sixteen Working members, eight external members and four nominated members).

Committee of Lloyd's

The sixteen working members of the Council of Lloyd's constitute the Committee of Lloyd's. The Committee is required to elect a Chairman and two or more Deputy Chairmen.

Corporation Departments

The Council/Committee are supported in their work by permanent staff of some 2,000. Some of these also provide a direct service to members of the Market.

Security behind a Lloyd's policy

Premium Trust Fund

Under the provisions of the United Kingdom Insurance Companies Acts, 1958 to 1982, underwriters are required to pay the whole of the premiums received by them in respect of their underwriting business into a trust fund out of which claims and expenses are met.

Underwriting Deposits

Every underwriting member before election is required to lodge with the Council of Lloyd's deposit consisting of cash, approved investments or a bank or insurance company guarantee/letter of credit as security for the fulfilment of underwriting commitments.

Premium Income Limits

The volume of business members may accept in any year is calculated at specified ratios of their Lloyd's deposits and qualifying means. If the premium income of members should exceed their premium limits, they must provide further deposits in proportion to the amount of overwriting and may be required to show increased means.

Underwriting Reserves

Most underwriting agents require their members to establish underwriting reserves in addition to their Lloyd's deposits. These funds may be in the form of personal reserves held in trust by the agent or in the case of the Special Reserve Fund in joint trusteeship with the Corporation of Lloyd's and is approved by the Inland Revenue.

Unlimited Liability

All underwriting members are liable in respect of the risks undertaken by them to the full extent of their private wealth.

Lloyd's Central Fund

Individual members are liable for their own underwriting commitments and should the assets held on their behalf at Lloyd's and their personal resources prove insufficient to meet their liabilities, the resources held centrally by Lloyd's are available to meet their obligations.

The Solvency Test

The United Kingdom Insurance Companies Acts, 1958 to 1982, require all Lloyd's underwriters to submit each year to a solvency test which must be conducted by a qualified accountant approved by the Council of Lloyd's.

Managing and Members' Agents

Members' agents

A member's agent undertakes the recruitment of new Names, the administration and servicing of existing names, and the compliance with the various regulations and requirements which affect their Names.

Managing agent

Each syndicate at Lloyd's is run by a managing agent. Some managing agents may be responsible for several syndicates of similar or different classes.

The underwriter manages the underwriting box and the agent manages the administration of the syndicate and is responsible to and for all the Names who participate in the syndicate.

Lloyd's Brokers

Contracts of insurance at Lloyd's cannot be effected directly between the insured and the Lloyd's underwriters. They can only be transacted through Lloyd's Brokers who are subject to the overall control of the Insurance Brokers (Registration) Act 1977. Sections 3(3) and 4(4) of that Act grant Lloyd's brokers special rights concerning registration and enrolment while day to day control is exercised both by the Council and Committee of Lloyd's and by the Lloyd's Insurance Brokers' Committee of the British Insurance Brokers' Association.

The principals of any firm desiring to be admitted as Lloyd's brokers must satisfy the Council and Committee of Lloyd's as to the solvency of their firm as well as their competence and familiarity with the Lloyd's market.

The one outlet rule states that a Lloyd's broker must be able to demonstrate, and be able to continue to demonstrate, that it can reasonably expect not to be unduly reliant in any one financial year upon any one body corporate carrying on insurance business or any one Lloyd's syndicate in the placing of its business.

With the exception of the acceptance of risks and issuance of documents under binding authorities and some services in claims negotiations and issuing certificates in motor insurance the broker is always the agent of the insured in Lloyd's transactions. All the common law duties of disclosure and utmost good faith apply to brokers as well as insureds in contracts of non-marine insurance at Lloyd's, while for marine contracts these duties are made statutory by the Marine Insurance Act 1906.

Market Associations

Associations representing respectively:–
Marine underwriters (Lloyd's Underwriters' Association)
Non-Marine underwriters (Lloyd's Underwriters' Non-Marine Association)
Aviation underwriters (Lloyd's Aviation Underwriters' Association)
Motor underwriters (Lloyd's Motor Underwriters' Association)
Underwriting agents (Lloyd's Underwriting Agents' Association)
Lloyd's brokers (Lloyd's Insurance Brokers' Committee of BIBA)

MENTAL REVISION QUESTIONS

1. Which market at Lloyd's produces the greatest premium income?
2. What is the minimum age for membership of Lloyd's?
3. What is a Special Reserve Fund?
4. What is meant by the term "external member"?
5. What is the premium trust fund?
6. What is the purpose of the Central Fund?

7. What are the main functions of members' and managing agents?
8. What are the primary requirements to be a Lloyd's Broking firm?
9. What is meant by the "one outlet rule"?
10. What is the function of Lloyd's Underwriting Agents' Association?

Chapter IV

LLOYD'S MARKET PRACTICE

i) THE METHOD OF CONDUCTING BUSINESS IN THE ROOM INCLUDING BROKERS AND SYNDICATE NUMBERS AND PSEUDONYMS.

PROPOSAL FORMS, PHYSICAL AND MORAL HAZARDS

Proposal forms are used for obtaining information which an insurer requires before he can underwrite a risk. They are used in the Lloyd's market for household risks, motor and personal accident risks amongst others.

Questions on Proposal Forms

The matters to which the questions relate can be sub-divided as follows:–

The description of the proposer

Questions include the name, address and occupation. The address is a rating factor in motor insurance and may be in theft insurance.

The occupation is of particular importance in personal accident, motor and liability insurances.

The description of the subject matter of the risk

Underwriters seek knowledge of the risk proposed and ask certain detailed questions where they consider that the premium to be charged might be influenced by the answers given. The factors are termed "physical hazards". Physical hazards may also be checked upon by inspection, this frequently occurs in connection with an industrial risk.

Examples of Physical Hazards

Construction of a building for a fire risk whether brick built with a tiled roof or a wooden building with a bituminous felt roof.

The type of premises concerned for a theft risk, whether a high risk as for a jewellery shop or a low risk as in the case of a bakers shop.

Details of previous insurance history of the proposer
Questions ask whether the proposer has been insured before and if so on what terms.

Also whether an insurer has refused to renew a previous insurance or increased the premium.

The insurers ask whether or not there have been any previous claims.

Amount of sum insured or limit of liability
This is the maximum amount payable under the policy and is also used by underwriters when calculating the premium to be charged.

Declaration in proposal forms
On all proposal forms there is a declaration which the proposer signs which declares that to the best of his knowledge and belief the answers he has given are true and correct.

The character of the proposer
Underwriters are also concerned as to whether or not the proposer is strictly honest in his dealings with them and is careful regarding his property or employees, this is termed moral hazard.

Examples

Bad moral hazard—where the insured makes a fraudulent claim or deliberately destroys his property.
Poor moral hazard of an individual—carelessness resulting in many claims on insurers which could have been avoided by due care.
Good moral hazard—the strictly honest insured who takes all steps to protect his property.

THE SLIP

Most insurance at Lloyd's is transacted by the physical attendance of a Lloyd's insurance broker upon an underwriter at his box, requesting insurance cover. The written form of the request is called a "slip", on which are set out the type of insurance, sum insured, period, location, clauses and conditions, as applicable, and most of those other essential details found in an insurance policy, all heavily abbreviated. Underwriters tend to specialise and market leaders tend to emerge for certain risks. It is to one of these that a broker will go with his slip seeking a "lead", which is signified by the underwriter in question subscribing for a proportion or percentage and signifying the various terms, conditions, and rate of premium. Subsequent underwriters on the slip are bound by these terms and rate of premium.

The first original underwriter becomes the leading underwriter for the insurance even though a subsequent underwriter may accept a larger proportion. The broker then takes the slip around the market until the total amount or percentage required is subscribed or underwritten—the literal meaning of to subscribe or to underwrite.

Such is the practice. The law is that, at Lloyd's a contract of insurance binding on the underwriters to cover the risk in question is made when an underwriter initials the slip presented to him by a Lloyd's Broker in the manner described and the slip contains an attachment date, i.e. a date at which the risk commences. Should a loss occur, underwriters subscribing to such a slip are in general terms bound to honour the lines they have subscribed, even though the broker has not completed his placing. When that slip is completed for 100% or any other required proportion of the risk with no amendment of the terms, cover is complete since those initialling have bound themselves to issue a policy under the terms demanded by that slip, if it contains an attachment date.

On occasions the slip, during the placing broker's passage round Lloyd's underwriting room, has changes made by successive underwriters from the original terms agreed by the leading underwriter. A following underwriter could insert amendments to the slip, which the leader and all other preceding underwriters should be shown and agree by initialling these subsequent amendments. In the event that a broker is unable to obtain such agreement and is therefore unable to complete a slip on the amended terms, two slips on different terms, each covering part of the same risk, may have to be prepared by the broker for the respective underwriters.

Nevertheless a slip containing an attachment date should not generally speaking be altered (except for minor corrections or clarifications) if the terms have been accepted by the insured, without the insured's prior consent.

In cases where 100% of the insurance is not subscribed and there is no other placing, then the insured is his own insurer for the unplaced balance. In marine insurance this situation is covered by Marine Insurance Act 1906, s. 81, and elsewhere the policy conditions should take care of this position.

The importance of the standard slip emerges from what has been stated above, namely that when initialled by an underwriter a contract of insurance comes into force between the insured and the syndicate(s) concerned. Slips vary as to form in minor details but, as an example, the main headings for non-marine placings will include:

Type	Whether fire only, fire plus additional perils (in which case those perils are detailed), public liability and so on.
Form	Here is stated which policy form is to be used with qualification or variation of perils if applicable.
Insured	Name, address and/or business, occupation
Period	The term of the insurance
Interest	This is a technical term meaning subject matter e.g., buildings, stock, machinery
Sum Insured or Limit of Liability.	The limit of indemnity
Situation	The location of the risk or territorial limits.
Conditions	Brokers will sometimes insert the special conditions they seek to have included, e.g., a small excess, while underwriters may impose conditions of their own before initialling the slip, e.g., a much larger excess.
Premium	Sometimes brokers will insert the rate they know the clients will accept—again underwriters agree or amend accordingly.
Brokerage	This is usually expressed as a percentage of total gross premium by brokers and varied or not by underwriters as the case may be.
Information	Here the broker should insert those material facts which he feels vital although his duty is fully to disclose all, often verbally.

Slips are enclosed when documents are to be submitted to Lloyd's Policy Signing Office (LPSO). Clearly, the correct compilation of the slip is vital since if the slip is wrong, the policy is wrong. The standard format of the slip is intended to assist not only the underwriter giving consideration to the risk, but also the policy drafter in the broker's office and those responsible for checking the policy and accounting for the premium at the LPSO.

Reference has been made to the "Information" section provided in the slip and to the broker's duty to disclose fully all material facts. The broker needs to be well briefed with additional facts and figures and must have available all relevant material such as survey reports, maps, plans, detailed claims records and any other documents or information which may have a bearing on the risk. The broker is required to assemble a balanced and accurate representation of the risk and should anticipate, as far as possible, questions which are likely to arise. If however, a question is asked to which the broker does not know the answer, it is his duty to say so and refer back for further information. The need to disclose every material fact must always be borne in mind. Many a disputed claim has turned upon brokers' alleged failure to disclose adequately such matters as past claims experience, and this is an area of grave concern in the market.

It is customary in the marine market for the broker to prepare a signing or "off-slip" from the original slip or open cover signed by the underwriters. The need for this procedure arises if, for instance, various options are expressed in the original slip or open cover, or if the original slip is for a whole fleet of vessels whereas separate signings are required for each vessel.

The off-slip must be initialled by the leading Lloyd's and company underwriters.

In the non marine market, if off-slips are used then agreement must be contained in the original slip and similarly the off-slip must be initialled by one or more of the leading underwriters.

Lead underwriter

Where it is necessary that a risk be spread among a number of syndicates, to prove acceptable to other subscribing underwriters the lead underwriter or leader must have the confidence of the other underwriters. To know which leader to approach first is an important part of the Lloyd's broker's expertise, although it does not follow that the first underwriter approached will necessarily lead the slip. Clearly, where large amounts are to be insured and many syndicates have to be involved, there is less opportunity for competition. For the smaller risk the broker may find the keener rate or better terms by shopping around. The lead underwriter is not necessarily the one who can write the biggest line, though normally he will write a substantial line.

The initialling of the slip by the underwiter is the acceptance of the insured's proposition. At the same time he agrees that in due course LPSO will sign a policy on his behalf in accordance with the slip when the policy has been prepared and submitted by the broker.

The signing of a policy may take place even after loss, and the underwriter cannot refuse to allow the policy to be signed on the ground that the broker failed to tender it with a reasonable time after the initialling of the slip. As has been stated, the initialling of the slip constitutes a contract which is binding.

The Committee of Lloyd's and market associations insist that policies must be signed within a reasonable time.

Renewals and alterations

When a risk is renewed it is customary to approach the same underwriters and to negotiate with them again. If, however, the broker and the underwriters cannot agree the broker will approach other underwriters in an effort to secure the terms he seeks, but he may need the leading underwriter's permission to do so.

If there is any material change in the risk while the policy is running it is usually necessary to secure the agreement of the underwriters on the risk, and obligatory where the policy so provides.

Binding Authority

A binding authority is an agreement under which a "coverholder" (usually a firm of insurance brokers) is authorised in accordance with the terms and conditions laid down therein, both to accept risks on behalf of those underwriters at Lloyd's subscribing to the agreement and to issue documents evidencing cover which bind those underwriters without their prior approval. A "Limited

Binding Authority" allows the coverholder to issue documents evidencing that risks have been accepted on behalf of underwriting members only after they have been accepted (and rated if appropriate) by the leading underwriter as provided on the slip.

The issuance of binding authorities is to facilitate the placing of business in the Lloyd's Market. The system of granting binding authorities is particularly advantageous in dealing with small routine business both in the United Kingdom and overseas.

The coverholder is not permitted to delegate his authority to another party without the prior written approval by underwriters.

The coverholder must be approved in accordance with regulations made by the Committee and the binding authority must be registered (and, if renewed by the underwriters, re-registered) in respect of every coverholder authorised thereunder at LPSO.

The policy

Once the slip has been written for 100% of the risk, the broker who has taken it round the Room returns it to his employers, the Lloyd's brokers concerned with placing the risk. It is the responsibility of that firm of Lloyd's brokers to produce the documentation, that is to say the policy (which they must draft, calculating the premium), the slip, plus a Premium Advice Note, and pass all to Lloyd's Policy Signing Office (LPSO). LPSO checks the policy in accordance with the slip, signs and embosses the policy and returns it to the firm of Lloyd's brokers concerned.

To legalise the insurance policy documents, the document is signed by the insurer. Lloyd's policies differ from those issued by insurance companies in that they are signed by LPSO on behalf of the participating underwriters. A list of syndicate numbers showing the percentage of the risk underwritten, is attached to the policy by LPSO staff. An essential clause is included in the policy, known as the Attestation Clause, which specifies the extent of each underwriter's commitment to the risk insured.

Central Accounting

The Corporation of Lloyd's (under whose control LPSO operates) provides a central accounting function which simplifies the Accounting Agreements between the broker and the underwriters.

MOTOR DIRECT DEALING

Since 1965, when Committee approval was given, motor syndicates have, in addition to their normal dealing with Lloyd's brokers on motor business, also increasingly dealt directly with non-Lloyd's broking companies in the U.K. This method enables syndicates to compete for personal motor insurance business with insurance companies having local branches.

The Council and Committee of Lloyd's lay down certain requirements to govern the transaction of 'direct' motor business at Lloyd's. These include, inter alia:

(a) the completion of a mandatory form of agreement between the Lloyd's broker and the Lloyd's syndicate which requires that all premiums must be paid through the intermediary of the Lloyd's broker who guarantees the payment of all such premiums to underwriters.

   Alternatively, such premiums may be paid to Underwriters either directly by the non-Lloyd's broker concerned or directly by the insured by means of credit card or bank direct debit. In respect of direct payments by the insured, however, the Lloyd's broker is not responsible for guaranteeing such payments to Underwriters.

(b) motor syndicate auditors being required to report on forms, which are provided to the syndicates by the Brokers Department, that an agreement in the mandatory form, referred to above, exists in respect of each direct motor arrangement.

Not all Lloyd's brokers handle motor insurance or operate in the direct motor field. However, those who do usually introduce the non-Lloyd's broker and, after the usual formalities and enquiries are completed, the non-Lloyd's broker will be provided with proposal forms, cover note books and rating and underwriting guide and will then deal directly with the syndicate concerned. This does not permit the non-Lloyd's broking companies to have access to the syndicates in the Underwriting Room at Lloyd's.

Lloyd's brokers are required to report annually to the Council regarding their direct motor business and in some detail if such business exceeds 10% of their total premium income, excluding life.

Lloyd's brokers are not permitted, without prior sanction of the

Council and Committee, to introduce in any one year direct motor business from any one outside agent in excess of 5% of the total premium income in that year from all classes of business, excluding life, of the Lloyd's broker concerned.

The amount of direct motor business individual Lloyd's brokers are permitted to accept overall from outside agents is limited to 60% of the total premium income in that year from all classes of business, excluding life, of the Lloyd's broker concerned unless prior dispensation is obtained from the Council and Committee of Lloyd's.

WHEN AN UNDERWRITER IS ON RISK

This subject needs to be broken down into two phases. The first is the time of an Underwriter's commitment to the contract of insurance, and the second is inception of cover under the contract.

Normally, an Underwriter is committed to the contract at the moment he subscribes his line to the slip. In cases where slips are over-subscribed, and all lines are "signed down" pro rata, the final extent of an Underwriter's commitment is not determined until the broker completes the placing operations and ceases to add lines to his slip.

Sometimes, for example when a broker is not certain that he has a firm order, a slip is placed "Subject to acceptance, no risk", the letters "SANR" or "SANR Ldr" being written on the slip. Under these circumstances, whilst Underwriters are committed to the contract the assured is not, and no risk attaches to Underwriters until the assured confirms the order to his broker and the broker has so advised Underwriters, or, more usually, the leader.

The attachment of the contract itself is governed by its wording; it may be a specified date or it may be an event such as the sailing of a vessel, the birth of a thoroughbred foal or the launching of a satellite.

The contract wording also defines the relationship between the period of the contract of insurance itself, and the timing of accidents for which it will respond. For example, a private motor car policy will respond for claims arising from accidents occurring during its (usually 12 months) currency. A products liability insurance, covering a manufacturer against liabilities arising out of faults in his products, may well respond for claims actually made against the

83

manufacturer during the policy period, regardless of the date of his negligence or the discovery of the consequences of events which happened long before the inception date of the policy.

It should be noted that if an Underwriter subscribes a line to a slip subsequent to the attachment date, and unknown to the insured or his broker, an event giving rise to a claim has already occurred, the Underwriter is on risk and must pay the claim.

UNDERWRITERS' REFERENCES

Wide variations of methods are used by different syndicates for their system of references.

Example of System

Purpose

a) to enable underwriters to control the gross premium volume and the outwards reinsurance volume of the Syndicate;

b) to enable underwriters to distinguish between profitable and unprofitable business so that they can develop profitable lines of business, and either correct or cut-back on unprofitable lines of business.

c) control of aggregation of risk.

System—Major Divisions

Syndicate divided into major divisions, each division should be carefully budgeted.

Individual References

Each division contains individual references.

The purpose being:–

a) To enable the underwriter to control the volume of individual sections of the major division;

b) To enable the underwriter to distinguish between profitable and unprofitable sections of the major division.

Usage

When an underwriter inserts his reference it must not exceed twelve characters and any blank spaces before or in the middle of a reference should be completed using the digits X or O or any other digit acceptable to the syndicate.

The reference is written in the space provided in the syndicate stamp which underwriter uses on the original slip.

SYNDICATE PSEUDONYMS

Each Lloyd's syndicate is issued with a unique number by which that syndicate is identified, and this number is used for all Lloyd's accounting purposes. When an Underwriter subscribes a line to a slip, he adds an initial as authority and his syndicate number to identify the syndicate, and this is transferred onto all documentary and computer entries.

As it is essential to avoid errors in copying or keying in these numbers, each syndicate is also given a unique three letter pseudonym for use in addition to the syndicate number. Lloyd's central accounting computers are programmed to reject any entries where the number and the pseudonym are not compatible, making it almost impossible for an entry to be processed to the wrong syndicate.

BROKER'S LPSO NUMBER AND PSEUDONYM

A Broker's L.P.S.O. number and pseudonym are allocated to each Lloyd's Broker by Technical Services Department, L.P.S.O. Chatham, for identification, validation and accounting purposes.

The Broker's L.P.S.O. number consists of three digits and the pseudonym of two or three letters.

The Broker's L.P.S.O. number and pseudonym have the purposes of acting as an identification for all accounting between the broker and Underwriters within the Lloyd's Central Accounting and as a unique identification and reference for each Broker.

Thus they enable the L.P.S.O. to check the validity of the broker's entries being processed and allow for quick and accurate sorting of documents at the L.P.S.O. Reception Barrier for return to the relevant Broker.

The Broker's L.P.S.O. number and pseudonym must be shown accurately on *every* document submitted to L.P.S.O., as failure to do this will cause delay.

Certain Brokers' organisations are allocated several Broker's L.P.S.O. numbers and pseudonyms and it is essential that the same number and pseudonym be used on all documents relating to the one item.

ii) THE WAY IN WHICH A POLICY IS PREPARED AND PROCESSED.

NON-MARINE AND AVIATION POLICY FORMS AND WORDINGS

A contract of insurance at Lloyd's is made between two parties, the insured and the Underwriters. The Broker is the intermediary acting on behalf of the insured to effect the insurance with the Underwriters.

The policy is the document evidencing the contract of insurance effected between the two parties. It sets the extent of the cover given by the Underwriters. To do this, it must set forth clearly and precisely the nature of the contract and contain all the terms, conditions, stipulations, limitations and warranties as agreed at the time of placing the insurance.

Some important factors to be remembered by the broker when preparing the slip in the Non-Marine market are:–

1) That the cover should exclude war and kindred risks as set out in the War and Civil War Risks Exclusion Agreement.
2) Underwriters have undertaken not to write financial guarantee business.
3) Life cover can only be written by certain syndicates and is limited to short term contracts.
4) The insurance may require the attachment of a Radioactive Contamination Exclusion Clause, mandatory on all but a few classes of risk.

There are certain basic requirements essential to be expressed in the policy, namely:–

1) Full name and address of the insured.
2) Consideration or premium for the contract.
3) Term or period of the insurance.
4) Amount of the insurance.
5) The description of the property insured and the location and perils insured against.

To legalise the insurance policy, the document is signed by the insurer. Lloyd's policies differ from those issued by insurance companies in that they are signed by L.P.S.O. on behalf of the participating underwriters. A list of the underwriters, showing the percentage of the risk underwritten, is attached to the policy. An essential clause is included in the policy, known as the Attestation Clause, which specifies the extent of each underwriter's commitment to the risk insured.

The terms and conditions upon which the insurance is granted must be expressed in the policy; these fall into two classes: General and Specific.

The general conditions are those which are common to the class of insurance and are usually printed on the policy form. Specific conditions are added either by being typed directly on the policy or by being attached to the policy by means of an attaching endorsement. Under the normal rules of construction for a legal document (and the policy is such a document) all conditions, alterations, etc. which are added specifically to the policy override any general conditions printed in the policy, the reason for this being that the specifically endorsed condition or alteration is deemed to express the particular intention of the contracting parties.

Thus it is essential that whenever possible the policy is issued on the standard printed policy form and within Lloyd's it is essential to know not only which standard forms are available for each class of business, but also the nature of the coverage afforded by the printed form.

The policy of insurance does not need to be expressed in any special form, but long experience and custom has resulted in certain standard forms of basic wording being used and these are usually printed.

In the Non-Marine market, the standard Lloyd's forms and clauses are prepared by the Non-Marine Association. The variety of forms is extensive and provision is made for specific versions for use in overseas situations.

The Non-Marine Association issues manuals containing all the forms and clauses. These are identified by title and by a reference number. The manual is divided into broad classes of insurance and the index enables forms or clauses to be found by title or reference number.

Forms and clauses approved by the N.M.A. can readily be distinguished by the statement printed thereon that it is "a form approved by the N.M.A.''. Any other printed form or clause must not contain these words.

The procedure for the Aviation market is identical with that for the Non-Marine except that the authority for purely Aviation forms and clauses is vested in the Lloyd's Aviation Underwriters' Association and a different printers code number prefixed by AV— is printed in the bottom left hand corner of forms and clauses issued and approved by the Lloyd's Aviation Underwriters' Association.

It is accepted that no specific agreement is required from underwriters where insurances are written in the Non-Marine market and forms and clauses approved by the Non-Marine market are being used for the purpose for which they were drafted. However, Standard Slip rules require that in the case of the policy forms used, a reference to it must appear in the appropriate position on the slip.

If a wording or form different from the standard N.M.A. wordings or forms is required, reference must be made thereto on the slip. If the form is an Underwriter's private printed form it may be used only for that Underwriter and unless that Underwriter has a line on the slip, the printed wording must not be used for other Underwriters without the express approval of the sponsoring Underwriter.

The Special Wordings Scheme was introduced several years ago as a means simplifying the checking of policies for certain risks for which special wordings are required. Special wordings may be required because there is no standard NMA or other market form or because a particular underwriter or broker wishes to use a special wording for the type of risk involved. Wordings within the scheme are usually sponsored by underwriters (although a few are sponsored by brokers or jointly by a particular broker and underwriter). Each wording is referenced "L.P.O." or, since January 1984, "L.S.W." with an identifying number.

Once a wording has been confirmed between the sponsor and L.P.S.O. as meeting the criteria of the scheme, stereotyped copies are made available to the market from Lloyd's Policy Office (The Carlton Berry Co Ltd). Each bears an L.P.S.O. "logo" and it's reference number. Wordings remain as first confirmed for an indefinite period unless amended by their sponsors. Brokers' or underwriters' private wordings which have not been brought into the Special Wordings Scheme may be used provided the wording is specifically referred to in the slip and a copy of the wording agreed by Underwriters is either attached to the slip or is on file for the broker at L.P.S.O.

Agreements for private wordings cannot be open-ended and are normally given for periods of 12 months and Underwriters review the wording with the broker before an extension of time is given. Underwriters will not normally agree to a private wording which is basically the same as a standard N.M.A. wording.

Certain clauses in common use but for which there is not sufficient demand to justify the cost of issuing printed clauses are available on file at L.P.S.O. It is not necessary for Underwriters to initial such clauses (e.g. PIPE STOVE Clause).

Underwriters private forms and wordings are also reviewed annually and are kept on file at L.P.S.O.

It assists L.P.S.O. if private forms and wordings, whether they be for Underwriters or Brokers, are re-submitted with renewal agreement without waiting for L.P.S.O.'s request for sight of renewals.

Thus, the general position may be summarized as:–

The standard procedure is that all insurances placed are signed on approved forms, clauses and/or wordings. L.P.S.O. is required to see that this procedure is carried out and to obtain through the Broker, approval for any form, clause and/or wording (other than those approved by Underwriters' Associations or those of private Underwriters) from the Underwriter(s) on the risk.

The provision of basic forms and clauses does not itself complete the preparation of a policy of insurance and it is necessary for the person responsible for preparing the policy to have a good working knowledge of the type of insurance being dealt with, what conditions and provisions appear in the printed form, what these mean and what to do to modify or amend them to suit any special requirements of the risk being handled.

MARINE FORMS AND INSTITUTE CLAUSES

S.G. (Commonly understood to mean "Ship and Goods")

Until 1.1.81 the S.G. Form was the only standard Marine Form in use in the London Market. Its origins date back over 200 years to the coffee house days of Edward Lloyd and its original use was for wooden sailing vessels. It uses old-world phraseology which appeared in the first schedule of the Marine Insurance Act 1906 and which is adapted to meet modern day requirements by the addition of overriding and complementary clauses. Each word has been tested in the courts and its meaning fully established.

The Policy face may be divided into four sections:

a) Assignment—i.e. whom the policy is in the name of and/or assigned to.

b) Duration of Risk:– Tailored for a voyage beginning "at and from" and ending "24 hours after vessel safely moored at anchor." this section also contains an Implied Sea Worthiness Warranty "Good Ship" and customary calling provision permission "to touch and stay at any ports or places whatsoever or wheresoever" ... as long as the calling is reasonable and necessary.

This is followed by a space for the Interest to be identified.

c) Perils:– includes marine perils i.e. perils of the seas etc. and war perils. This section also includes a Sue and Labour Clause and a Free of Capture and Seizure Clause which is a war exclusion clause added in italics in 1898 in order to exclude war risks giving the underwriters the right to include or exclude war risks and charge extra premium if so desired. The Free of Capture and Seizure Clause excludes more war perils than are acutally mentioned.

This is followed by a space for the "rate" or "premium", the policy being in effect a receipt for the premium, and a memorandum clause which states that small claims will not be paid in certain circumstances.

d) Attestation clause:– an agreement by underwriters to participate "each for his own part" in the risk.

MAR FORM (MAR being Marine)

Introduced since 1.1.82 following pressures to replace to S.G. Form by the United Nation conference on Trade and Development (UNCTAD). The pressures to change revolved around the thought that "the immortalisation of an antiquated and obscurely worded document as being immune from any improvement is excessive and unnecessary and that consideration should be given to altering the method of granting (marine) insurance coverage from the 'enumeration of perils' method to an 'all risks' grant of coverage with specific exceptions."

The MAR Policy itself offers no coverage; cover therefore must be provided in the clauses attached to the policy which have been agreed on the original placement. It merely contains an attestation clause, a policy schedule which provides for details of the insurance and a statement "subject to English Jurisdiction" on the face. It has been designed along with new clauses in precise, easily understandable language. The clauses used to expand/restrict the cover under the S.G. Form should not be used with the MAR Form and the clauses for use with the MAR Form should not be used with the S.G. Form.

MAR Policy Clauses

Cargo clauses A, B and C

All the new cargo clauses follow the same format, the main sections being:

1) The Risks Covered
2) The Exclusions
3) The Duration
4) Claims

Clause A covers "All Risks" subject to the exclusions provided in Section 2 whereas clauses B and C are Named Perils Clauses in that they name precisely what is covered and not covered.

Institute War Clause (Cargo)

The format is similar to cargo clause A and it states exactly what war perils are included whereas S.G. War Clauses are used to include war perils excluded by the Free of Capture and Seizure clause in the marine Policy. Piracy is no longer a war peril but a marine peril.

91

Institute Time and Voyage Clauses (Hulls)

The hull clauses also take basically the same format and are all named perils clauses clearly setting out the perils and coverage provided.

Both hull and cargo clauses state English law and practice to prevail and they also include many of the elements previously contained in S.G. policy form, for example a Sue and Labour Clause has been specially included in the clauses.

In addition to the S.G. and MAR Forms there are a number of other policy forms in common use:

a) Slip Policy form (LPO 212 A); is used where agreed (and in accordance with the slip policy scheme rules) if a full policy is not required to be issued. Many facultative Reinsurances are signed on a slip policy.

b) "J" and "J(a)" forms; these are non marine forms with a minimum of conditions so that appropriate wordings can be attached or used in the marine market for various types of insurance for which the marine form is not appropriate e.g. marine liability risks.

c) Some underwriters have their own private forms for use on certain classes of business and insurance forms and clauses of other nationals are also frequently used.

INTERPRETATION OF POLICIES

There are certain rules which are applied to the interpretation of a policy, these are:

a) Added clauses take precedence over printed wordings where at variance with the same.
b) Any ambiguity in wording is construed against the underwriters in favour of the assured.
c) The terms of the contract must be given their ordinary meaning but custom is accepted to explain what is not clear.

In reading a policy there is a recognised procedure for alterations and attachments made to the same. This is:
a) Handwritten wording takes precedence over all other

b) Typewritten wording follows handwritten in order of precedence

c) Rubber stamped wording is next, followed by

d) Printed clauses and

e) Clauses printed in the margin of the policy.

MOTOR INSURANCE DOCUMENTATION

Apart from proposal forms and policies, the main types of document used in motor insurance are

a) Certificates of motor insurance

b) Cover notes

c) Green cards

Certificates of Motor Insurance

Certificates of motor insurance are required by law to be issued as evidence that there is a policy of insurance in force covering the use of the vehicle on the road, as required by the Road Traffic Acts. The certificate of motor insurance is no more than evidence that the minimum cover required by law is in force and does not show that the insured has Third Party only or Third Party Fire and Theft or Comprehensive cover. A certificate may also be contained in a cover note, renewal notice or special document pending issue of the final certificate.

The certificate is divided into a number of sections describing the following:

a) The registration details of the vehicle insured, but many motor syndicates issue "blanket" certificates which state that the vehicle insured is any vehicle owned by the insured or hired to him under a hire purchase agreement. Syndicates adopt this wording so that a new certificate does not have to be issued each time the insured changes his car. The insured is warned by a notice on the certificate that he must notify underwriters of any change of vehicle as soon as reasonably possible after the change.

b) The name of the insured

c) The period for which the certificate is effective

d) The persons who are insured to drive the vehicle in accordance with the relevant policy.

e) The use to which the insured vehicle may be put in the terms of the relevant policy and the uses which are specifically excluded.

There then follows an attestation to the effect that the policy to which the certificate relates is issued in conformity with the Road Traffic Acts of Great Britain and the corresponding legislation in Northern Ireland and the Channel Isles. Finally, the certificate is signed by an authorised representative of syndicate.

Motor Temporary Cover Notes

These are documents issued as evidence that insurance cover has been granted, pending issue of a policy. There is usually a time limit of 15 or 30 days. The motor cover note must include a certificate of insurance to comply with Road Traffic Act requirements.

Cover notes may also be issued in the event of a change of vehicle when a blanket certificate has not been issued or where there is some other major change in the insured's existing cover or a change in the class of use covered by the policy. Cover notes must show the time and date on which cover commences and must never be back-dated.

Green Cards

Green cards are used as evidence of minimum insurance cover in most of the countries of Western Europe and are instantly recognisable to the police and other authorities in European countries. A British motorist who takes his car abroad is always well advised to carry a Green Card. This is so even though the 1972 EEC Directive on the Insurance of Civil Liabilities Arising from the Use of Motor Vehicles has theoretically made it unnecessary for motorists travelling abroad to have a Green Card as their policies are now automatically extended to provide the minimum cover required by the laws of the countries which have signed the relevant agreements. It must be emphasised that a Green Card is simply proof that the minimum cover required by law is in force. It does not mean that the policy cover which the insured normally enjoys in the United Kingdom has been extended to apply in full to Europe. To obtain in this extension the insured must specifically request it from his underwriters and pay the additional premium involved.

Motor Renewal procedures

Renewal procedures in motor insurance differ from those applied in other classes of insurance due to the existence of compulsory insurance and the need to issue a certificate of insurance. Because a certificate must be issued, renewal papers (including the certificate) must be drawn up a few weeks in advance of the actual renewal date. The broker passes the renewal notices received from underwriters to individual insureds.

Motor insurance renewal procedures differ from those in other classes firstly because there are no "days of grace" allowed for the payment of motor renewal premiums. The premium must be paid on or before the due date or the cover expires on that date. However, because there may be an unavoidable delay in the payment of the premium to the insurers (for example, the insured's remittance is delayed in the post) or for some other reason (for example, there is a change of vehicles just before renewal date, necessitating a change in policy conditions). Thus it is customary for insurers to print on the back of their motor renewal notice a 15-day cover note and temporary insurance certificate to ensure that the insured who intends to renew his policy and who has paid, or is paying, his renewal premium, remains fully protected. Such temporary cover notes are not used in other classes of insurance. The cover note and temporary certificate give only Road Traffic Act cover.

BROKERS POLICY DEPARTMENTS

Once the broker has placed the risk and issued the cover note, the policy must be prepared.

A broker will normally have a policy department, and a Reinsurance Broker will have a contract wording department. The purpose of both departments is to interpret and elaborate on the details and conditions contained in the placing slip.

The broker's responsibility is to construct the policy or contract wording from the clauses agreed by the parties in the original placement—the finished policy document being the legal document which may be necessary for the collection of a claim particularly in respect of marine business.

The policy on completion will normally be forwarded by the

broker to his client although he may sometimes be asked by the client to look after the policy in case a claim may be submitted.

LLOYD'S POLICY SIGNING OFFICE

The original function of the group of Departments known as 'L.P.S.O.' was fairly obviously, the signing of Lloyd's Policies. At the beginning of the present century Lloyd's Policies were still being signed by individual Underwriters in the Underwriting Room. The Broker's Slip had originated long before that and a system had evolved whereby a Broker having got his slip written (i.e. initialled by Underwriters willing between them to accept the whole risk), returned to his office and had a policy prepared based on the conditions of the slip. The policy and slip were then delivered to and collected from the boxes of one Syndicate after another in order that the Underwriter, or his clerk, having satisfied himself that the policy agreed with the slip that had been initialled, impressed on it a stamp showing the names and shares of the members of the syndicate, inserted his line, and added his signature.

This was a time consuming method and the state of the document when it was finished left much to be desired. As a result, in 1916, a group of Underwriters set up an office to undertake the tasks of checking policies prepared by Brokers against the slips which they, the Underwriters, had initialled, signing the policies on their behalf, and finally advising them of details of policies which had been signed in this way. Lloyd's Underwriters' Signing Bureau, as the office was called, was originally an office run by Underwriters independently and its use was a matter of choice, but in 1921 the Corporation of Lloyd's took over the administration and in 1924 it became mandatory for Lloyd's policies with a sum insured of more than £100 to bear the L.P.S.O. Seal. The name of the office was changed to Lloyd's Policy Signing Office in 1927.

With the passage of time, L.P.S.O. has been required to undertake numerous other duties including the checking against the Broker's slip of endorsements to the policies, both those involving changes of premium and those where no change is concerned.

Developing directly from the necessity to advise Underwriters of policies signed on their behalf and premiums payable to them, came a series of methods of providing this information, each more sophisticated than its predecessor, until the introduction in 1955 of the present system of punched cards and tabulations which provides Underwriters with more information than ever before, infomation which enables Underwriters to make the numerous returns necessary, both those required by the Committee of Lloyd's and others required by Government Departments.

During the late 1950 and early 1960's the L.P.S.O. extended its activities to include the taking down and advising to Underwriters on punched cards of Marine and Non-Marine Claims and Refunds and Syndicate Reinsurances.

These were all steps leading to a final goal which Lloyd's had been working towards for many years—that of Central Accounting.

Prior to 1961 Underwriters were supplied by L.P.S.O. with details of premiums payable and claims due but the actual cash transaction took place between firms of Brothers and Underwriting Syndicates individually—that is at that time about 260 firms of Brokers and 400 Underwriting Syndicates. Under the Central Accounting System, in addition to producing cards and tabulations for Underwriters, figures are accumulated either on a weekly (for certain classes of business) or monthly basis depending upon the type of business being processed and Syndicates and Brokers are advised of one amount which is due either from them or to them in any particular week or month as a result of all the transactions concluded.

All money from Brokers and/or Syndicates is paid to the Market Financial Services Department who also distribute US and Canadian dollar amounts, settlements being carried out through the Lloyd's American Trust Fund and Lloyd's Canadian Trust Fund respectively.

The Computer Services Department, which carries out processing for L.P.S.O., based on the information supplied on Premium Advice Notes, Treaty Statements, claims forms and Debit and Credit Notes, originally formed part of L.P.S.O.

During recent years other Corporation Departments have begun to make use of the services the Computer Services Department is able to provide, and to reflect this change of emphasis the Department now forms part of the Systems & Communications Group.

The roles of L.P.S.O. can be summarised as:–

1. Checking of documents and associated functions carried out for underwriters
2. Operating central accounting
3. Roles carried out for the Committee/Council of Lloyd's (provision of statistical information, monitoring for regulatory purposes etc.)

The affairs of L.P.S.O. are directed by a committee, comprising nine members, who have delegated authority from the Council of Lloyd's.

The departments of L.P.S.O. are:–

Marine Department
Non-Marine Department
Special Schemes Department
L.P.S.O. London Group
Technical Services Department

Each of the first two of these Departments is responsible for the processing of policies and/or A.P./R.P. endorsements from receipt, through—

1. Checking in all its aspects, e.g. checking the provisions are what the Underwriters intended, that it conforms with Committee of Lloyd's requirements, that syndicates are current and valid for the type of business written, that premium calculations are correct.
2. Identifying with L.P.S.O. number and date, and
3. Signing the policy or stamping the endorsement.

Simultaneously information on the Premium Advice Note supplied by the Broker with each policy and/or endorsement and slip must be checked, completed with a narrative and have coded information added to it to provide an accurate source document for entering data from it and the slip by means of visual display units and transmission to Computer Services Department.

The information includes that necessary to enable Underwriters to fulfil Audit requirements, for example, and for the accumulation by the Computer Services Department of Foreign Legislation and Department of Trade and Industry requirements.

Special Schemes Department

The Special Schemes Department, was actually set up to deal with a number of different and quite unconnected procedures—the principal ones being:–
Contract Scheme
Non-Marine Claims/Refunds
"B" Scheme registrations
"T" Scheme registrations
Syndicate Reinsurances
and now in addition incorporates the Records and Amendments Section which is involved in the correction of all entries which for a variety of reasons have been incorrectly processed.

Part of this section is concerned with investigating, and analysing and generally sorting out queries from work whilst it is actually being processed through the Computer Services Department.
Many of the queries dealt with by Record and Amendments come in the first place through the Underwriters' Liaison Office which forms part of the L.P.S.O. London Group, and is the "front line" when it comes to receiving Underwriters' queries and complaints.

Technical Services Department

This Department provides a centre of technical insurance expertise for the benefit of Underwriters and Brokers and, of course, L.P.S.O. staff. The Department researches and negotiates in connection with the implementation of new schemes on requirements in so far as they affect L.P.S.O. and where necessary takes measures to maintain the standard of L.P.S.O. work.

It sets standards by which checking of documents is to be carried out and by monitoring the work actually done ensures that the necessary quality is maintained.

The Technical Services Department provides an advisory liaison service for Brokers on all matters other than technical insurance matters handled by the Checking Departments.

The department produces and maintains technical manuals for L.P.S.O. and market use; among these is the Lloyd's Policy Signing & Central Accounting Manual. The manuals are reviewed and where necessary reworded or reformatted to reflect the changing views and requirements of the market.

L.P.S.O. London Group

This group provides a liaison service between L.P.S.O. and the Lloyd's market. It also controls the receipt and despatch in London of documents submitted to L.P.S.O.; processes very urgent items and registers binding authorities.

THE ROLE AND RESPONSIBILITY OF BROKERS IN THE HANDLING OF PREMIUMS

In most instances an insurance with Lloyd's Underwriters must be placed by a Lloyd's Broker—the insured does not have a direct contact with the Underwriter. The Broker is the middle man in the contract of insurance between the Underwriter and the insured.

The Broker acts for the insured in accord with the law of Agency; the insured is the Principal and the Broker is the Agent and as such is responsible to the insured.

In consideration for the insurance the insured is required to pay a premium to the Underwriters and in the Lloyd's market this is transferred by the Broker. The Marine Insurance Act, 1906 provides that the Lloyd's Broker is directly responsible to a Lloyd's Underwriter for the Underwriter for the payment of premiums due, whether or not he has received it from the insured and by custom and usage this requirement has been adopted for all insurances at Lloyd's other than for direct debited motor insurance and business evidenced with a certificate in association with a binding authority. Since July 1972 payment of premium has become subject to trading terms between Underwriters and the Broker whereby the Broker is required to see that the premiums are transfered to the Underwriters within a specified period from the inception of the risk.

As a protection for the Broker who has made the payment of the premium to the Underwriter but has been unable to collect the premium from his client or insured, the MIA, 1906 grants the Broker a lien on the marine policy. A lien may be defined as a legal claim upon property until a debt on it is repaid.

Because the MIA, 1906, provides that the Underwriter is directly responsible to the insured for the amount which may be payable in respect of losses or in respect of returnable premiums,

100

the Act confers upon the Broker the right to retain the policy document until the insured pays him the premium. This lien is of some value because a claim must be physically endorsed on a policy and could not be collected by the insured who does not possess the policy. In addition the insured may require the policy to be lodged with a bank as security, or to pass to an assignee, or to send with a bill of lading to a consignee.

TERMS OF CREDIT SCHEME, TERMS OF TRADE SCHEME AND LATE SETTLEMENT REPORTING SYSTEM

One of the market practices at Lloyd's is that the broker initiates the central accounting "billing" procedure by having an entry "taken down" by the Policy Signing Office. This is unlike most commercial organisations, where the supplier of services normally initiates the charging procedure and follows up the collection of debts.

The Terms of Credit Scheme was developed during the 1970's under which, when each risk is accepted by underwriters, an agreed period of credit is negotiated, within overall limits which have been determined for each type of risk, country and currency, within which brokers can expect to account to underwriters for the premium.

The Terms of Trade Scheme was introduced in January 1987 and replaces the Terms of Credit Scheme for the Non-Marine market only. The recommended terms are markers which underwriters and brokers have agreed can reasonably be expected to be achieved in most cases for most of the time. The terms for each risk are negotiable in individual cases between individual underwriters and brokers as part of the rating process.

Having determined an agreed period of credit, the brokers' settlement performance is measured by comparing the agreed period with the date at which the entry is ultimately settled to the underwriters and the Late Settlement Reporting System reports brokers' overall settlement performance.

The system relies on information collected from each entry as it is processed through the Policy Signing Office and produces statistics showing the proportion of entries which are settled late compared with those which are not late. Although information is collected on both the value of entries and the number of items

101

involved, the most widely used performance statistics are related to value.

The late settlement performance of brokers is monitored by underwriters and by Market Financial Services Department.

In addition to action taken by individual underwriters at the box, the Committee of Lloyd's, through the Market Financial Services Department also plays an active part by taking appropriate action against those brokers with the worst performance overall and in individual markets.

CENTRAL ACCOUNTING

The aim of the central accounting scheme is to avoid the need for several hundred Lloyd's brokers to settle with several hundred Lloyd's syndicates. At its most basic level the objective of the central accounting scheme is for each broker and each syndicate to receive or pay just one net amount of premiums less claims in each accounts period, for each of the three accounting currencies used, viz; Sterling, US dollars and Canadian dollars.

Settlements occur monthly or weekly depending on the business involved.

However, in practice this principle has been eroded because of the need for urgent settlements in each of these three currencies covering premiums, claims and syndicate reinsurances. Also the principle is not followed for UK motor business and some overseas motor business which is excluded from the central accounting scheme.

The Computer Services Department produces accounting statements based on the entries processed through the Policy Signing Office and the actual cash settlement between brokers and underwriters is dealt with in the Market Financial Services Department.

For each item, detailed advice cards are produced for underwriters periodically during the month, together with a summary known as the "underwriters tabulation". Brokers do not receive advice cards but receive listings known as "brokers daily statements".

At the end of each week or month a consolidated statement is produced which includes those items previously covered on advice cards and daily statements which are due for settlement at the end of that particular period.

In addition to premium and claim items, the monthly settlement statement also covers a range of miscellaneous items where many syndicates/brokers are involved in order to reduce the need for individual payments. These cover such items as charging the running costs of the central accounting scheme to syndicates, collecting various levies and taxes from brokers and/or underwriters, and other similar items. Each of these is identified by a separate reference and is advised to the syndicates or brokers concerned in advance of being included in the settlement.

The monthly and weekly settlements are arranged in accordance with a calendar which is published each year showing the settlement dates for each of the threee currencies.

Cash Transfer Procedures

For any particular settlement, amounts due to or from each syndicate or broker are payable on the same day. This is arranged through a central bank account (one for each settlement currency) by the Market Financial Services Department on behalf of the Committee of Lloyd's. Wherever possible, direct debiting/crediting arrangements are made with banks used by the brokers and syndicates to ease this process. In the event of settlement being delayed, an interest charge is levied on brokers and syndicates.

THE ROLE AND RESPONSIBILITIES OF BROKERS IN THE SETTLEMENT AND PAYMENT OF CLAIMS

THE PROCESSING OF CLAIMS

Advice

The first notification of a claim can come from the insured or alternatively, from the producing broker. In the case of notification by an insured this is often given to the broker by means of a telephone call and it is essential to ensure that the personnel within the Claims Department, who are receiving that telephone call, should be aware of the basic details that are required from the Insured (i.e. date of loss, location of loss, nature of loss, if possible some indication of amount involved and also the telephone number of the insured or address where he can be contacted). Notification of a claim from a Producing Broker to the Lloyd's Broker can be by means of letter, cable or telex and should contain the above relevant details. In certain instances a Non-Marine Policy will contain a "Claims Notification Clause". This usually designates a specific adjuster to act in respect of all claims that arise under that policy and in such cases the first notification of a claim received by the Lloyd's Broker is usually received from the adjuster nominated in the "Claims Notification Clause".

It is of vital importance to ensure that the Insurers are advised of a loss with the utmost urgency so that they can ensure that their representative (i.e. the Adjuster) for non marine risks or the Salvage Association or a consulting surveyor for marine risks is appointed without delay. (The Salvage Association is an independent body and acts on behalf of any party who instructs it.) In many cases of direct business the insured needs to be continually advised of the progress of his claim.

Reinsurance

There are many instances where the Lloyd's Broker who places a risk is requested to arrange certain reinsurances by the Insurers that have accepted that risk. In consequence of this it naturally follows, that when the Lloyd's Broker advices the original Insurers of a claim he must at the same time, advise the Reinsurers.

Payment

The market is selling a service and the most vital part of that service is the speedy and efficient settlement of a claim. The claims' personnel of brokers' offices must always be able to assess priorities in order to achieve a prompt settlement. This will help the firm to retain its existing business and possibly attract new business.

Lloyd's Underwriters' Claims and Recoveries Office (L.U.C.R.O.)

The Claims Section

The Claims Section deals with claims and refunds on behalf of the majority of Marine Underwriters at Lloyd's. The section is responsible for both direct and reinsurance claims and being divided into three specialist areas (namely Hull, Cargo and Reinsurance) is equipped to handle losses arising on a wide spread of risks, including Non-Marine, Aviation and oil exploration and production, subscribed to by the Marine Underwriters for whom it acts. The Office has absolute and unlimited authority from more than 90% of the Marine Underwriters to settle claims on their behalf.

It is also L.U.C.R.O's responsibility to ensure that Underwriters are made aware of any advices that it sees in order to put them in the position of being able to assess their outstanding claims. This is done through a Computer System known as O.M.C.A.S. (Outstanding Marine Claims Advice Scheme).

The section will often be involved in a claim from the early days of its development because, once the Broker has been informed of a casualty he will advise L.U.C.R.O. of the details and obtain an relevant instructions from them. Thereafter L.U.C.R.O. will be contacted as necessary with additional information, and give further instructions on a wide range of problems which may include not only matters directly concerned with minimising the loss or presentation of the claim, but also, in the case of a casualty involving a third party, taking correct steps to ensure the preservation of any right of recovery arising from a hull claim are pursued by the insured, whilst recoveries relating to claims dealt with by the Cargo Section are passed on to, and pursued by, the Recoveries Section.

The Recoveries Section

The Recoveries Section acts on a "no cure no pay" basis for Lloyd's Marine Underwriters, and Insurance Companies both at home and abroad, in the exercise of their subrogation rights, and works closely with the Cargo Claims Section and the Salvage Association.

105

Recoveries are pursued against bailees of cargo (e.g. ship-owners, airlines, warehouse keepers, inland hauliers, etc.) and other third parties, based either on a breach of the terms of a contract or on a failure to exercise the appropriate standards of care imposed by law. Refunds or recoveries obtained are disbursed to the appropriate principals less charges.

In addition, the Section protects cargo interests in relation to General Average and Salvage and issues Corporation of Lloyd's General Average Guarantees. Settlements are made under such Guarantees and collections effected from the Insurers concerned. The Section is also authorised to settle General Average Contributions and Salvage claims submitted by Lloyd's Insurance Brokers.

Lloyd's Underwriters Non-Marine claims Office

The object of L.U.N.C.O. is to provide the market with a quick and efficient advice of claims/agreement to settle service. In many cases brokers are enabled to make a single presentation for all L.U.N.C.O. members (en masse), other than the leader, with considerable saving to underwriters and brokers in time and work detail.

Membership of the scheme is open to all Lloyd's underwriters who write non-marine business.

Basis of operation

A broker must prepare a claims file which includes a synopsis sheet and advise the leading underwriter whether a L.U.N.C.O member or not before L.U.N.C.O can deal with a non-marine claim. Furthermore, in the case of an unsigned slip the broker must prepare a continuation sheet, showing all Lloyd's underwriters signed lines, syndicates and references in slip order, as before signing no record of this information exists in L.P.S.O. Details of the claim and policy details are checked and advice cards are sent to underwriters. All losses advised through the L.U.N.C.O. office are numbered and dated for reference, 40 being added to the date i.e. 1st July 1971 becomes 41st July 1971. This is to distinguish them from the paid claims processed by the L.P.S.O. All increases, decreases, settlements, reports etc., on claims previously advised to L.U.N.C.O. are shown to L.U.N.C.O. following presentation to the leader. This ensures that the up-to-date situation on any claim is advised promptly to all underwriters, normally within 2–3 days.

L.U.N.C.O. is also able to produce Claims Outstanding lists to brokers which reduces the need and size of outstanding lists from underwriters (i.e. one list from L.U.N.C.O. to each broker instead of a separate list from underwriters to each broker.)

Underwriters obtain a narrative card of losses in which they are involved, (above their noting levels). These cards present to underwriters all the details that appear on the claims advice sheet.

Each quarter underwriters receive a tabulated list, showing all their outstanding losses in Underwriting reference order and in year of account. This has also been divided into the four currencies of U.S. Dollars, Sterling, Canadian Dollar and Convertible currency. They also receive a list of their involvement in designated catastrophies.

Lloyd's Aviation Claims Centre

Lloyd's Aviation Claims Centre was formed in 1965 with the object of improving the speed and efficiency of aviation claims handling within Lloyd's. Lloyd's Aviation Claims Centre offers a complete claims service which includes the prompt advising of claims to members by way of computer produced cards. In addition to providing these cards the Centre also provides a quarterly record to members (in either printed or magnetic tape form) detailing the claims in which the member is involved together with claim reserves. With few exceptions the Centre handles every aspect of claims from first advice to conclusion.

Although including the word "Lloyd's" in its title and enjoying the approval and co-operation and assistance of the Corporation and Committee of Lloyd's, the Centre is run and financed entirely by its member underwriters.

Motor Claims

Claims are handled by motor syndicates at their offices. On being advised of an accident or other occurrence which may give rise to a claim, the first action of a broker or the syndicate's claims department should be to issue to the insured a claims form, the

insured should also be asked to pass on to the insurers, unacknow-
ledged, any communication which they may receive from a third
party. This is because the insured may prejudice the insurer's
position if he attempts to deal with third parties himself.

Many motor insurers use a series of claims settling agreements,
whose objective is to speed up the settlement of claims and reduce
claims handling expenses. Examples are the "knock for knock"
and "third party sharing" agreements.

v) THE ROLE AND RESPONSIBILITY OF UNDERWRITING STAFF AND THE SYSTEM OF DELEGATION AND RESPONSIBILITIES WITHIN AN UNDERWRITING ORGANISATION

The role and responsibility of the appointed Underwriter of a
syndicate have already been studied. In carrying out his duties, the
Underwriter is supported by box staff, the size of which may vary
from two or three to as many as a dozen or more. But large or small,
the essential functions are very much the same.

Before outlining the operation of the delegation of responsibility
within an Underwriting organisation, it is important to appreciate
the vital importance of a system of delegation being disciplined and
efficient. Firstly, whilst the conduct of business at Lloyd's is, if not
casual, certainly of an informal nature, nonetheless, a simple
misjudgement can literally cost a fortune. Secondly, if everyone
involved in the underwriting for a syndicate follows one set of
guidelines, any errors in those guidelines will become apparent
and can be corrected, but without that discipline it is very hard to
identify the cause of problems, yet alone correct them.

Every Underwriter has at least one person, in addition to himself,
who actually underwrites new business at the box. In a small
syndicate, it may be that only the Deputy Underwriter has been
given this authority, and then only in the absence of the Underwriter. In big syndicates writing very broad accounts, there may be
several assistant Underwriters all underwriting full time, usually
each specialising in a particular class of business such as Hull,
Excess of Loss, Treaty, etc.

More junior members of a box staff, not yet competent to
underwrite new risks but having a sound understanding of the
syndicates business, may be authorised to agree, by initialling

brokers agreements, minor amendments to risks, declarations off covers and so on.

The negotiation and agreement of claims, whilst within the overall responsibility of the Underwriter and contentious matters are referred to him, is subject to considerable delegation. Some large syndicates have specialist claims staff dealing only with claims, in small boxes claims are dealt with by underwriting staff in addition to their other duties. In addition, all marine, non-marine and aviation syndicates, to a greater or lesser extent delegate claims matters to their respective market's claims offices (LUCRO, LUNCO and LACC).

The next responsibility of box staff is record keeping, including keeping records of all risks written, and the premiums received and claims paid thereunder, including sorting entries out into classes for the purpose of statistical analysis, whether it be by entry in books, coding items for computer operators to deal with, or keying directly in at a terminal on the box.

Syndicate records are maintained for many purposes, regulatory and so on, but the most important purpose is to enable Underwriting staff to gauge the effectiveness of their underwriting, and to make any necessary corrections promptly. To this end it is the responsibility of all Underwriting staff constantly to monitor the statistical records they keep, and where appropriate, to ensure that their colleagues are kept fully informed.

vi) THE NATURE AND IMPORTANCE OF MARKET AGREEMENTS.

MARKET AGREEMENTS

There are a number of different Market agreements entered into by Lloyd's underwriters and/or Insurance companies, whereby insurers undertake to adhere to a specific course of action or understanding. The agreements are generally intended to facilitate the processing of business or maintain the solvency of insurers. They may also arise from national or international legislative requirements. There are many agreements covering a number of subjects. These can be divided into Market Wide agreements, Single Market agreements and Committee of Lloyd's agreements.

Market Wide agreements are entered into by both Lloyd's

underwriters and Insurance companies, for example the War and Civil War Risks Exclusion Agreement between Lloyd's and BIA (now ABI), which was brought into effect in 1937 and re-issued on 1st April, 1982, following a major revision. The current Agreement provides that insurers will exclude loss, damage or liabilities resulting directly or indirectly from war and civil war from all insurances and re-insurances other than those excepted classes listed in the Agreement. The list of excepted classes to which the Agreement does not extend includes, for example, life and personal accident and professional indemnity insurances. War and civil war may be included in marine hull policies, subject to the terms of the War Risk on Hulls Agreement, in Marine Cargo Policies, subject to the terms of the War Risk Waterborne Agreement.

Boards set up by Lloyd's and the insurance companies deal with questions arising out of the Agreement and applications to amend the list of excepted classes.

AGREEMENTS LIMITED TO A SINGLE MARKET

Agreements limited to a single market extend across only a single market, that is, marine, aviation, or non-marine. They may be joint agreements between Lloyd's Underwriters and insurance companies. Examples of such agreements include the use of leading underwriters' clauses in all three markets, the Companies Collective Signing Agreement (non-marine), and the marine "Waterborne" agreement (which reinforces the war and civil war exclusion agreement insofar as cargo business is concerned).

The original Leading Underwriters' Agreement (NMA) was introduced in 1936 and revised in 1965 to facilitate the handling of changes in individual insurances without the need for the broker to see all underwriters subscribing to a risk. The Agreement lays down four categories of matters which must be shown to all underwriters and provides (with certain reservations) that all other matters need only to be seen by the two leading Lloyd's underwriters. This agreement was drawn up and is administered by the NMA.

The Companies Collective Signing Agreement (CCSA) (Non-Marine) was introduced in 1965 and a large number of insurance companies in the London market participate. It authorises the leading CCSA Company to sign a collective policy on behalf of all other CCSA Companies on the risk, thus considerably reducing the number of signatures needed. The Agreement provides an indemnity to the leading company against any liability incurred as signatory which would not otherwise have been incurred if the policy had been individually signed by all companies. In addition, a number of schemes have been introduced by Lloyd's underwriters aimed at facilitating the processing of business at Lloyd's and these have required market agreements to authorise their operation. Examples include schemes to simplify the processing of non-marine claims, small claims, small additional premiums and return premiums, and treaty balances.

COMMITTEE OF LLOYD'S AGREEMENTS

Certain Committee of Lloyd's decisions to protect the solvency of the Market have been implemented by underwriters. One such arrangement is the voluntary agreement entered into by Lloyd's underwriters whereby underwriters have agreed not to underwrite direct Financial Guarantee business. Reinsurance of approved Insurance companies may be underwritten by specialist credit syndicates, subject to certain safeguards.

vii) THE PARTICULAR RESPONSIBILITIES OF LEADING UNDERWRITERS WITHIN THE LLOYD'S SYSTEM INCLUDING THE OPERATION OF LEADING UNDERWRITERS' CLAUSES

For the great majority of its marine, non-marine and aviation business, Lloyd's relies on the subscription system, that is to say a single insurance is shared amongst a group of syndicates, each taking a proportion of the risk in return for receiving a similar proportion of the premium.

For such a system to work, it is necessary that all Underwriters subscribing to one insurance give cover on identical terms and rate of premium. To achieve this a broker obtaining insurance cover for his client must find a group of Underwriters all willing to accept a share of the insurance on the same terms, and those terms must be the best available. This could not be achieved by starting negotiations from scratch with each syndicate approached, so the

111

system has evolved under which the broker obtains quotations from one or more Underwriters whom he knows to be competitive in that class of business and having found the one most attractive for his client, will seek support for those terms from other Underwriters.

The Underwriter whose quotation is accepted is known as the Leading Underwriter, or leader, and the broker's ability to persuade sufficient other Underwriters to follow that lead depends very much on the confidence other Underwriters have in the leader's knowledge, ability and method of conducting business. It is central to the whole Lloyd's system, therefore, that leaders in their actions should take account not only of the interests of their own syndicate, but also those of the syndicates who follow them.

This responsibility of leaders goes much further than the initial fixing of the terms of the insurance; at that stage at least, following Underwriters have the option of writing a line or leaving it alone. It is when some alteration is made to a risk, and it is particularly difficult for one of many following Underwriters to stand out against a majority who accept the alteration, that a leader must consider the interests of those who follow his lead.

Some insurances are subject to many amendments, additions or extensions during their currency, and unless there is some particular arrangement, all alterations have to be agreed by every Underwriter subscribing to the slip. To ease the broker's workloads, devices known as Leading Underwriters Clauses are incorporated in many broker's slips. These take various forms, but all fulfill the same purpose of, subject to various restrictions, authorising the leader to agree alterations not only for his own syndicate, but also on behalf of the other syndicates on the slip. The simplest—and with Underwriters least popular—form of Leading Underwriters Clause permits the leader to agree almost anything; some require the first two or three Underwriters on the slip to agree before the following Underwriters are bound, and the most sophisticated clauses spell out in considerable detail the extent of the leaders' authority.

Whilst Leading Underwriters agreements are necessary for speed and efficiency, it is very important that their convenience should not be abused. Different syndicates have different Underwriting strategies and systems, different capacities and different reinsurance protections. It is therefore incumbent upon both leaders and brokers to ensure as far as humanly possible that Leading Underwriters clauses are not used to bind following Underwriters to agreements they might otherwise decline, and that following Underwriters are always advised to any significant matters agreed on their behalf.

Leading Underwriters' responsibilities extend into the area of claims, where although each individual syndicate can legally agree or refuse to agree a claim the influence of the leading syndicate is very great. The different markets have different practices, but all contain various provisions for notification or agreement of some claims by leading underwriters (or a number of leading Underwriters) and the relevant market claims offices.

It is the duty of brokers to be familiar with the requirements of these schemes and to comply with them.

viii) THE IMPORTANCE OF PROMPT AND EFFICIENT TRANSFER OF PREMIUMS AND PAYMENT OF CLAIMS

Any form of business involves money, and very broadly the money of a business may be divided into two parts. The first part is money in use, be it income from the sale of products or services, expenditure on raw materials, wages etc. or money invested in buildings, machinery etc. The second part is money kept in reserve for extraordinary expenditure, such as buying new equipment or covering trading losses.

For an underwriter, the money in use includes incoming premiums, outgoing claims and administrative expenditure and provision for claims yet to be met on current and expired policies. The second part of an underwriter's money, often referred to as the solvency margin, is the base upon which he can run the risks inherent in offering insurance protection. The bigger the solvency margin, the more risks he can run and the more business he can accept, increasing his total trade and hopefully, profit.

However, the first call on an insurer's money is to make provision for claims. If premiums are received late, he will have to make the necessary provision out of reserves, thereby reducing his solvency margin, and with it his ability to trade. Prompt payment of premium is clearly most important for this reason alone.

A more obvious advantage is that with existing high interest rates, the sooner insurers receive their premium, the longer the period they can have it invested, increasing their investment income. This enables insurers to offer more competitive rates.

In international business, fluctuations in currency exchange rates have a considerable effect on an insurer who accounts in sterling. Whilst the effects are not necessarily adverse, it is an area outside the control and expertise of insurers, and they much prefer to have their money in their accounting currency as soon as possible.

Finally, on the subject of premiums, there is a credit risk attaching to any outstanding debt, and in general the risk increases with the length of time a debt is outstanding.

On the subject of claims, prompt payment is simply good business practice. The right to a claim is the commodity the insured is purchasing, and an insurer who does not pay a proven claim promptly is selling shoddy goods. In the case of domestic insurance it is largely a matter of irritation—to be without a car because you haven't the money to buy a replacement whilst insurers delay paying a claim is infuriating. In business, particularly small businesses, the ability to earn a living may be suspended until money is available to replace lost or damaged equipment. Prompt payment of claims is an essential element in insurance protection.

ix) THE IMPORTANCE OF PROMPT AND EFFICIENT HANDLING OF CLAIMS

The prime reason that an individual or company buys an insurance policy is that he or it identifies the possibility of pecuniary loss or liability. Should such a loss or liability occur, a claim will normally ensue and the insured can expect a prompt indemnification of this loss to avoid any further financial suffering.

In these circumstances the prompt and efficient collection and handling of claims is essential, not only to re-imburse the insured but also to maintain the good reputation of the underwriter to settle the claim within the terms of the policy.

In submitting the claim to the underwriter, the broker will first ensure that his client has fulfilled his obligations regarding the premium payment. He will then interpret the policy conditions and present the claim to the underwriter's claims representative.

Whilst most claims fall within the policy terms there are those where the broker has to display further skills in persuading underwriters as to the original intention of his client.

114

When the claim is agreed, the normal process of Lloyd's Central Accounting system comes into play. When underwriters agree to a special settlement, this agreement will have the effect of speeding up the payment by the underwriter to the broker and it is then the undoubted responsibility of the broker to pay the insured immediately on receipt of these monies.

The efficiency of a broker's business is more readily measured by the effectiveness of the actions of staff in dealing with claims, and the basis of such efficiency must be a good recording and filing system so that papers and information are speedily extracted.

The reputation of the Lloyd's Market can be damaged by slow payment of claims. The United States market is particularly sensitive to slow payment of claims and certain powers exist in that country to compel prompt payment.

The trading conditions and standards, particularly in the United States, but also worldwide have become more complex and it is vital for the continued prosperity of the Lloyd's Market that all within the Lloyd's community recognise this fact and the changes which have taken place over the last few years.

The London Market, and in particular that of Lloyd's, has been synonymous with financial integrity, thus it must continue to provide a claims servicing capability that is beyond reproach.

There should always be prompt acknowledgement of the insured's claim, prompt investigation, prompt advice to the claimant of the result of the investigation of the claim, and, if valid, prompt payment of the claim.

Everyone in the chain leading to claims settlement has a part to play in ensuring that the handling is efficient and prompt. Proper briefing from one person to another in this chain can assist in minimising delays or preventing any delay.

Lloyd's has impeccable security thus prompt handling of claims can only enhance the position.

REVISION NOTES

PROPOSAL FORMS

Proposal forms are used for obtaining information which an insurer requires before he can undertake a risk. They are used in the

Lloyd's market for household risks, motor and personal accident risks amongst others.

Slip

Precis of risk providing all relevant information.
—forms basis of negotiation between Broker and Underwriter
—indicates Underwriter's acceptance
—provides proof of cover till policy issued.
—contains information for Brokers and L.P.S.O. as to premiums and endorsements

Off slips

It is customary in the marine market for the broker to prepare a signing or "off-slip" from the original slip or open cover signed by the underwriters.

The off-slip must be initialled by the leading Lloyd's and company underwriters.

In the non-marine market, if off-slips are used then agreement must be contained in the original slip and similarly the off-slip must be initialled by one or more of the leading underwriters.

Lead underwriter

Where it is necessary that a risk be spread among a number of syndicates, to prove acceptable to other subscribing underwriters the lead underwriter or leader must have the confidence of the other underwriters. To know which leader to approach first is an important part of the Lloyd's broker's expertise.

The lead underwriter is not necessarily the one who can write the biggest line, though normally he will write a substantial line.

Alteration

If there is any material change in the risk while the policy is running it is usually necessary to secure the agreement of the underwriters on the risk, and obligatory where the policy so provides.

Direct Motor Dealing

Syndicates may deal with non-Lloyd's broking intermediaries in the UK subject to requirements laid down by Council and Committee.

When an underwriter is on risk

Normally an underwriter is committed to the contract at the moment he subscribes his line to the slip, however the attachment of the contract is governed by its wording.

Broker's L.P.S.O. number and pseudonym

Allocated to brokers for identification, validation and accounting purposes.

Underwriters' Pseudonyms

The three letters serve to validate the syndicate numbers which identify the syndicate and is used for all accounting purposes.

Underwriters' References

Purpose

a) to enable underwriters to control the gross premium volume and the outwards reinsurance volume of the Syndicate;
b) to enable underwriters to distinguish between profitable and unprofitable business so that they can develop profitable lines of business, and either correct or cut-back on unprofitable lines of business.
c) Control of aggregation of risk.

Must not exceed twelve characters.

Policy forms

The policy is the document evidencing the contract of insurance effected between the two parties. It sets the extent of the cover given by the Underwriters. To do this, it must set forth clearly and precisely the nature of the contract and contain all the terms, conditions, stipulations, limitations and warranties as agreed at the time of placing the insurance.

Wordings

1. L.A.U.A. and N.M.A. standard wordings and Institute Clauses for Marine risks.

2. Underwriters' own wordings
3. Brokers' own wordings
4. Wordings individually negotiated.
5. "Special" wordings

Non-Marine Policies

There are certain basic requirements essential to be expressed in the policy, namely:–
1) Full name and address of the insured
2) Consideration or premium for the contract
3) Term or period of the insurance
4) Amount of the insurance
5) The description of the property insured and the location and perils insured against.

Marine Policy forms

The MAR Policy form and clauses

The MAR Policy Form is simple, clear and no longer contains terms of insurance. The policy, which contains a schedule incorporating those requirements under the M.I. Act 1906, is a vehicle to carry the necessary clauses which are self sufficient.

Motor Documentation
Certificates of Insurance

Required by law to be issued as evidence that there is a policy of insurance in force.

Motor Cover Notes

Evidence that insurance cover has been granted pending issue of a policy, usually subject to a time limit of 15 or 30 days.

Green Cards

Evidence of minimum insurance cover in most countries of Western Europe.

Lloyd's Policy Signing Office

The functions of L.P.S.O. are the checking and signing of Lloyd's policies and accounting for monies passing between Brokers and Underwriters.

Terms of Credit Scheme, Terms of Trade Scheme and Late Settlement Reporting System

The Terms of Credit Scheme was developed during the 1970's. When each risk is accepted by underwriters, an agreed period of credit is negotiated within the overall limits which have been determined for each type of risk, country and currency.

The Terms of Trade Scheme was introduced in January 1987 and replaces the Terms of Credit Scheme for the Non-Marine market only. The recommended terms are markers which underwriters and brokers have agreed can reasonably be expected to be achieved in most cases for most of the time. The terms for each risk are negotiable in individual cases between individual underwriters and brokers as part of the rating process.

Having determined an agreed period of credit, the brokers' settlement performance is measured by comparing the agreed period with the date at which the entry is ultimately settled to the underwriters and the Late Settlement Reporting System reports brokers' overall settlement performance.

Central Accounting

The aim of the central accounting scheme is to avoid the need for several hundred Lloyd's brokers to settle accounts with several hundred Lloyd's syndicates. At its most basic level the objective of the central accounting scheme is for each broker and each syndicate to receive or pay just one net amount of premiums less claims in each accounts period, for each of the three accounting currencies used, viz; Sterling, US dollars and Canadian dollars.

Marine claims

When the Assured has informed his Broker of a casualty, the Broker will advise L.U.C.R.O. of the details and obtain any relevant instructions for them. Thereafter, L.U.C.R.O. will be contacted as necessary with additional information, and give further instructions including matters directly concerned with minimising the loss or presentation of the claim, and also, in the case of a casualty involving a third party, taking correct steps to ensure the preservation of any rights of recovery.

Non-Marine Claims

Membership of L.U.N.C.O. is open to all Lloyd's underwriters who write non-marine business. The object of L.U.N.C.O. is to provide the market with a quick and efficient advice of claims/agreement to settle service.

Aviation Claims

Aviation Claims are dealt with by the Lloyd's Aviation Claims Centre on behalf of its member syndicates and it offers a complete claims service.

Market Agreements

There are a number of different Market agreements entered into by Lloyd's underwriters and/or Insurance companies, whereby insurers undertake to adhere to a specific course of action or understanding. The agreements are generally intended to facilitate the processing of business or maintain the solvency of insurers. They may also arise from national or international legislative requirements. There are many agreements covering a number of subjects. These can be divided into Market Wide agreements, Single Market agreements and Committee of Lloyd's agreements.

Market-wide agreements are entered into by both Lloyd's underwriters and insurance companies.

Agreements limited to a single market extend across only a single market, that is, marine, aviation, or non-marine. They may be joint agreements between Lloyd's Underwriters and insurance companies.

Certain Committee of Lloyd's decisions to protect the solvency of the market have been implemented by underwriters agreeing to abide by agreements proposed by that Committee.

Prompt tranfer of premiums

If premiums are received late provision for claims will have to be made out of reserves thereby reducing the solvency margin of the syndicate also Underwriters are deprived of the investment earnings from money which is rightfully theirs.

Leading underwriters' agreements

Purpose is, subject to various restrictions, authorising the leader to agree alterations not only for his syndicate but also on behalf of other syndicates on the slip.

Prompt payment of claims

Need for prompt payment to retain existing accounts.

Prompt handling of claims

The reputation of the market can be damaged by slow payment of claims, it must provide a claims service capability that is beyond reproach.

MENTAL REVISION QUESTIONS

1. What is the purpose of a proposal form?
2. What is the procedure if off-slips are used in the non-marine market?
3. When is an underwriter on risk?
4. What is the purpose of underwriters' references?
5. What are the purposes of the Terms of Credit and Terms of Trade Schemes?
6. What is the objective of the Central Accounting System?
7. Why does the Lloyd's Market have Market Agreements?
8. What are syndicate pseudonyms?
9. What are the essential requirements to be expressed in a non-marine policy?
10. What were the main reasons for the establishment of Claims Offices?